How to Meet, Date and Marry Your Filipina Wife

BY PETER CHRISTOPHER

ISBN: 0989900916
ISBN 13: 9780989900911
Library of Congress Control Number: 2013948902

FOR MORE INFORMATION
ABOUT YOUR FREE READER BONUS, VISIT
www.globalfiance.com/philippines
TODAY!

Table of Contents

CHAPTER ONE

Good Guys Deserve Good Girls

I have an encouraging message for all you men out there…

If you are single, I want to help you meet the soulmate of your dreams!

For many of us, finding a long-term companion and sharing our lives with them is one of the most exhilarating and emotionally rewarding success stories there is.

But trying to accomplish it with a beautiful person you met on a dating site makes that dream a very difficult proposition.

Despite the odds, it is a very honorable goal. A Filipina woman is worth your time, effort and resources because she will be blessed by God just for you.

I want to help you make it happen. I want to help your dream come true.

If you are the type of man who believes in true love and is looking for a woman of good character and who shares your values and will love you for them, then read on.

There is no need for you to be single much longer, my friend.

The information I share with you in this book will help you chart a course toward being with the Good Girl you deserve. When we were growing up, we always knew who the good girls were in school. They were the girls we wanted to bring home to our mother.

They were the marrying type. They had character, kindness, loyalty, sincerity and were as unselfish as a soup kitchen at Thanksgiving.

They loved their family.

Well, guess what?

Filipina women have those exact same qualities, and most of them have those beautiful brown eyes, too. These are the 21st century version of the good girls we used to know.

And, one of them is waiting to meet fall in love with you.

Over the past five years, I have helped thousands of guys just like you meet the love of their lives. We did so by creating a *website* that links sincere single men from all countries of the world with wondrous women from the Philippines.

You will read incredible accounts of some of these men and their wonderful Filipina wives in the following pages. They are not just success stories, they are real. We know that a cross-cultural marriage can work, and will do everything in our efforts and expertise to make it work for you.

All that you read here is true. Honestly, you don't need a website to meet a great lady but using a quality website like ours will certainly make things easier.

I encourage you to follow the simple plan that I have outlined in this book – what to do and what to avoid – in the international world of dating. There are a lot of unethical and illegitimate sites out there which take advantage of good guys like yourself.

This book is for any sincere man who wants to consider the possibility of a future life with a wonderful Filipina woman. I do, however, admit that I have a particular expertise gained by running a business focused on providing what I consider a Christian environment to make initial connections. So for those of you who are not accustomed to Bible verses or my particular beliefs – don't worry, this book will be great for you too.

However, you should all know that Filipina women are almost across the board Christian women. And as such, I don't think it's out of place that I relate from time to time a verse or two, as I believe it is important for even a less devout man to understand this important side of a Filipina.

So I ask you to be honest and genuine in your search.

"Whoever walks in integrity walks securely, but he who makes his ways crooked will be found out." Proverbs 10:9.

Christian Filipina, the international dating business I founded seven years ago, is committed to character, not cash. The phrase, *"What Would Jesus Do?"* is our marching order. We not only want to serve you, we want to protect you, too. You are trusting us to find the romantic woman for your life.

We take that responsibility very seriously. My personal faith in Christ is the reason I created this ministry. I want Jesus to be immersed in its dating destiny every step of the way.

A little bit about me.

I was born and raised in the Northeast. My parents were liberal, unionized teachers who divorced when I was five years old. As a youngster, I had a hard time developing friendships. I believe it was because I took on my parents' anxieties and had difficulty conforming to the prevailing social norms.

I also had a tendency to be quickly and openly judgmental, which did not endear me to my classmates. You could say I was emotionally wounded growing up.

Throughout college and young adulthood, I had dozens of girlfriends. A few times, I asked some of them to marry me with mixed responses. But none of the engagements for those who said yes were ever acted upon.

Someone once said:

"Marriage is not finding the right person; it is BEING the right person."

Up to that time in my life, I had not been the right person so it really didn't matter who I dated or almost married. I simply wasn't ready.

I truly wanted to be married and raise a family, but I couldn't seem to find the right girl. More importantly, I couldn't seem to become the right guy.

At the age of thirty, I traveled to the Philippines. I had been invited by a former classmate's father who had grown up in that country and had told me it was a great place to do business.

So, I went.

It soon became apparent to me why so many older men frequently visited this island nation. The Filipina women were arguably, the most beautiful women in the world. The guys who traveled there ranged from gentlemen looking for a wife to sex tourists who were only looking for fun.

With a population of over one hundred million people and a younger demographic than most wealthier countries, (due to their large family sizes) there are a lot of single women throughout the country.

A lot of *gorgeous* single women.

Over time, I developed a vision for that business I wanted to begin: A godly website connecting sincere Christian men from all over the world to the good girls next door, who had little chance of ever living a quality life apart from their existence in a depressed Third World country.

I decided to call it — **Christian Filipina.**

The next step in my plan was to develop a mission statement that defined the ministry.

Our Ministry Mission Statement:

"We believe that people thrive in quality friendships, family and community, and that through sincere commitment to each other we most fully develop as human beings. In this healthy environment we grow and transform obstacles into

opportunities instead of running away from problems or emotionally bouncing around like pinballs.

We at Christian Filipina seek to help men and women with an interest or history in the Philippines to meet and grow together. We are a friendly and safe online community where good people can respectfully meet. We are a resource for our members over time as they continue to build friendships and family."

This book will help you decide whether or not to join our site.

90% of what you read here will be applicable to you and your desire to learn more about your romantic relationship with a Filipina woman, or any woman for that matter.

We wrote this book for Good Enough Guys. You don't need to be a movie star, a stockbroker, a professional athlete or a renowned public figure in any occupation. You don't need to have your own YouTube channel or Twitter account or be a powerful presence on Facebook.

You don't need to go to church every Sunday or consider yourself a strong religious person.

We are not looking for perfect men or upstanding Christians. We are interested in members who strive to be honest, hard-working and generous men. We hope you have some education, training or expertise in a line of work, whether you learned it in school, on the job or in your family business.

You are currently single, either never been married, divorced or widowed. Maybe you have had several long relationships or never been on a date in your life.

That's okay with us.

Just be a Good Guy with integrity.

Here is the good news for you as a Good Enough Guy. There are millions of Good Girls out there and they have been dreaming all of their lives to meet someone just like you. We will help you find them.

Then, you will see it is not too late to live happily ever after with the woman of your dreams by your side for the rest of your life.

I will give you the information and point you in the right direction. After that, you go out and fall in love. This is not impossible.

This is your romantic destiny.

CHAPTER TWO

What Works — A Model for Success

There are just a few critical steps you need to follow to succeed.

- ***You have to be ready.*** If you meet the right person, you need to be prepared to take the next step and be ready to change your life.
- ***You ought to meet several great ladies and spend time casually with them online.*** There is great value in getting to know several women before you focus in on one.
- ***When you find the right lady and you want to be together, you need to talk about and decide what the best next step is for both of you.***
- ***Live happily ever after!***

Let's consider these steps one by one.

You have to be ready. When you meet the right person, you need to be ready to take the next step. If you have a major psychological problem or cannot support yourself financially, work on that before you begin dating online. You don't have to be perfect or rich, but you must be able to afford a few round trip tickets to the Philippines (or elsewhere) and to pay for other expenses.

You can find your wife-to-be in the Philippines or just about anywhere in the world. But first, you need to be honest in asking the question: **"Am I ready to make a COMMITMENT?"**

The time to answer that question is before you meet someone, not after you have been with a woman who has already fallen in love with you. I believe that Christian Filipina is a great site to meet beautiful women with character. But, until you are truly ready to commit to one of them, be realistic with who you are first.

If you are emotionally ready, then sign up and let's get started!

You ought to meet several great ladies and spend time casually with them online. One of the easiest ways to start meeting people is to use an online dating service. There are literally thousands of international online dating services out there. Unfortunately, many of these sites are fraudulent. I will teach you how to deal with these obstacles later on in this book – how to identify a good site from a bad one and a real person from a criminal scammer.

Can you just skip the dating site and meet someone in person by visiting another country? Yes, it is possible, but for most men, using a reputable dating site is easier and cheaper. I truly believe that I have created a great site, but whether you choose ours or another one you need to sign up for a membership to start meeting people.

Here are some simple rules for getting the most out of your online dating experience:

- ***Rule Number One – Take some time to learn.*** It is unlikely that the first woman you meet online will become your soulmate. During your first month or two, have many conversations with members as friends using mail messages or webcam chats. Ask them about their family, country, language and faith. Tell them about yourself.

- ***Rule Number Two – Don't exchange contact details right away.*** Wait at least four to six weeks before sending any contact information (your personal email address, Skype ID, phone number, etc.) to the person you are communicating with on the site. If you pull the trigger too soon, the lady who is interested in exploring a relationship with you may think you are not sincere and distrust you. Why? Scammers try and lure their victims off-site as quickly as possible because it is easier to take advantage of people away from site security restrictions.

- ***Rule Number Three – Once you start meeting people you think might be good candidates, resist the urge to fall in love too soon***. It will probably take you several weeks or even months of steady online conversations with a lady before you are confident that she is a good candidate to be your one and only. If you move too fast you risk getting involved with the wrong person for the wrong reasons, wasting your time and money and, most important of all, limiting your chances of meeting your true love.

Try not to get emotionally involved with anyone until you meet them face-to-face. Until you actually see each other in the flesh, spend some time together and meet her family and friends (especially important in the case of Filipina women), there is no way to know with any degree of certainty that you are right for each other. Yes, it is true; many people become *very* emotionally involved before they meet in person. Yes, some of those relationships become successful lifetime commitments. My goal in this book is to share with you what I've learned over the years. It is simply a fact that in most cases, if you wait to start saying things like "I love you" and "I want to marry you" until you make the trip overseas to see your lady, you will be better off and you have greatly increased your odds of success.

- ***Rule Number Four – Don't waste your time, money or energy with scammers.*** Don't send money to anyone you connect with online who you haven't met first in person. If you make this mistake and later find out you were scammed, report it to the site management and chalk it up to experience. Some men become obsessed with scammers. They want to write books or make websites or videos proving that they were scammed. If you meet someone who tries to get you to send money to them (or someone else they claim is going to help you), don't do it! But if you do end up running into problems, don't beat yourself up over it or let it defeat you, just learn from the mistake and move on. The same goes if you have been a member of a scam site, such as those charging per-minute or per-message fees where the women are just actresses. Report it to the government right away and get back to meeting quality people.

- ***Rule Number Five – Evaluate your potential soulmate based on her values and lifestyle.*** Remember why you're dating online. It is certainly a legitimate goal to use an online dating service to make new friends and explore possibilities, but if you're reading this book, you are most likely looking for your soulmate. What types of qualities are you looking for in a wife? As you talk with various ladies, keep those qualities in mind. Do not fall into the all too easy trap of judging a potential partner by physical appearance alone. Stop and think: has this method of choosing a woman worked for you in the past? If it had, you probably would not be reading this book. Values count, qualities count, and character counts.

- ***Rule Number Six – Don't get stuck sending emails forever, get over there!*** Get your passport and plane ticket and get over there to meet some ladies in person. Once you have one or two (or more) ladies you think might be great to meet, it is time for you to get over there and meet them in person. If you don't have a passport, be aware that it takes several weeks to go through that process, so call up your local passport or post office and get your application filed. Then, pick a date and buy some tickets. (I will share with you later in this book the details on travel, what it will be like to meet her in person, the dos and don'ts, etc.)

When you do find the right lady and you want to be together, you need to talk about and decide what the best next step is for both of you. Engagement is very common, followed by one of you moving so that you can share your lives together. Most commonly our members become engaged or married in the Philippines and then file visa paperwork so that she can join him in his home country. However, we also have many members and friends who have chosen to live together in the Philippines instead, either temporarily or permanently. We will talk about these options and the visa process later in this book.

Live happily ever after! Men, this is what it's all about. Finding a wife overseas, bringing her home and having a happy life together is not a fantasy, it happens literally every day to guys just like you.

Many of you reading this book have already heard of the possibility of meeting your future bride overseas, even if it was just in the form of a joke. I am here to assure you that meeting the love of your life through a reputable international dating site is no joke – it's a very real possibility.

Good Girls still exist; in fact, there are millions of them just waiting to hear from you. By Good Girls, I mean women who have a strong personal morality, faith and desire to be married to the right man. Before you begin your journey to find your other half, I ask that you try and leave your Western preconceptions and prejudices behind. Many Western women have tossed traditional values aside in our materialistic, me-focused modern culture. You know this because you have dated them – and perhaps married one – only to end up lonely and divorced.

The women that you will meet by following the plan I lay out for you in this book could care less if you drive a Mercedes or wear Hugo Boss clothes or own your own business. They are looking for exactly what you are looking for: a faithful, hard-working, honest person to be their best friend, lover and soulmate.

The model I'm sharing with you works. You will find someone you love and who loves you too. You will find a woman that shares your faith and values.

Just ask Maxie and Joy Burchell, one of the many couples who met at the site that I started.

CHAPTER THREE

Success!

Maxie and Joy Burchell

Maxie Burchell comes from a small town in Arkansas. He owns and operates a chicken farm. Maxie wanted a traditional marriage with a woman of high integrity, someone he could both love and trust. Unfortunately, he was unable to find his true love in America.

Before Maxie became a member of Christian Filipina, he tried several other international dating sites with no success. Most of the ladies he met in the U.S. did not share his values or personal goals. He was ready to give up, both on dating sites and on the idea that God would send him the soulmate he had been praying for. Maxie was in his early fifties and had never married.

But Maxie did not give up and, as it turns out, that made all the difference.

In 2010, he discovered Christian Filipina and began meeting a large number of ladies online from the Philippines who shared his values and desire to be in a traditional, Christian marriage. He began to feel far more comfortable with the process of online dating and increasingly confident that he had found a site that worked for him.

Once he became an active member, the biggest challenge Maxie faced on the site was that he wanted to find a woman near his own age. While he had no prejudice against younger women and was open to being led by the Lord, Maxie really wanted to meet a wonderful lady who was fifty or so.

Maxie's prayer was answered the day he found Joy.

Right away Maxie knew that something special was happening. It wasn't long before he and Joy were talking on the phone and using Skype on a daily basis. Maxie is a quiet, reserved man who is deeply spiritual. Joy is an effervescent, cheerful lady with a great sense of humor. The old adage "opposites attract"  proved true in their case – they were both looking for exactly those qualities in a partner.

In 2011, Maxie went to the Philippines and met Joy and her family. As soon as they met face-to-face, they knew for sure that they wanted to be together forever. While it took fourteen months for Joy's visa to be processed, in 2012 she came to Arkansas, they were married and to this day, they are not only happy, but absolutely crazy in love. They are immensely grateful to Christian Filipina for providing the vehicle for them to meet and become husband and wife.

While it sounds like a fairy tale, both Maxie and Joy faced  their share of challenges before they were able to meet and get married. Distance, cultural differences and skepticism were very real obstacles in their dating experience. For Maxie, he had to overcome the old prejudice that online dating was a "second choice" for "desperate" people. For Joy, she had to get past her hesitancy and doubts about Maxie being the right man for her. They took their time, did it the right way, and are now being well rewarded for both their faith and prudence.

When you see them together – this devoted Asian wife and her head over heels in love American man – you can't help but think that this is a match definitely made in heaven (we have several interviews with Joy and Maxie and others available online at **www.globalfiance.com/testimonials** – check it out!).

Patrick and Venus Archibald

Patrick and Venus Archibald's story is one of unexpected love that became a reality through Christian Filipina and Marife, Venus's younger sister. Marife was Patrick's long-time online friend. Patrick knew that Marife had an older sister who was still single, so he dared to ask if it was okay to be introduced to her. Patrick was serious about finding his true love and believed that God blesses those who keep their faith strong.

When he found out about Venus in 2010, Patrick was thirty-two and divorced with a son. Venus was also thirty-two at the time that they met, but she was not very active on Christian Filipina. She recalls Marife asking her if she was interested in meeting her Christian Filipina online friend. She giggled when she saw Patrick's picture. Venus remembers telling her sister, "No problem! Look at his picture, he's so good looking!" There was a spark between them right from the beginning. "Venus is amazing. I was interested in getting to know her well. It just made me happy to talk with her," Patrick says today, thinking back to when they first met.

Venus was not in a hurry. She made sure that it felt right before she jumped into a relationship with Patrick. "I received three handwritten letters in the mail every month from Patrick, plus daily emails," Venus recalls. After three months of constant communication, they were ready to take their relationship to the next level.

In the summer of 2011, Patrick flew to meet Venus and her family in Santa Catalina, Negros Oriental. As soon as he saw Venus, he knew that God had answered his prayers. For two weeks, they talked about what their life might look like in the future. With five days left on his vacation, Patrick asked Venus and her father for her  hand in marriage. They agreed and everyone was happy. "I took her to the jewelry store and told her to choose which ring she liked. It was one of the happiest moments of our lives," Patrick recalls. The next day, he had to leave her, but promised that he would be back in eight months for their wedding. Patrick sent Venus money each month for the wedding preparations. They were married in the Philippines on December 2, 2011. In February of 2013, Venus arrived in Canada after fifteen months of waiting.

They were able to work around their differences in denomination. Patrick is a Baptist and Venus is a Catholic, but they said, "We decided to respect each other's faith and belief." They made the decision to spend a year taking turns each week either attending Catholic Mass or Baptist Sunday service.

They are now happily living together as husband and wife in Canada.

Prentice and Maria Worley

Prentice Worley is a retired United Methodist pastor and a widower with two sons. After forty-nine years of marriage, he lost his wife to cancer in August of 2008. His oldest son had been married to a Filipina lady for some time; in fact, Pastor Prentice had performed their wedding ceremony. Prentice had always admired his daughter-in-law's faith and dedication to her family, so after he had been alone for a few months, he decided to try and see if God might bring him a Filipina woman to love.

After more than one wrong turn down the road in terms of online dating sites, Prentice came upon Christian Filipina. Not long thereafter, he met Maria, the lady that would become his wife.

Maria is a Filipina girl with a sweet disposition and a heart of gold. When they met, Maria was working as a maid, cleaning condos and houses in Manila. She had only been in one semi-serious relationship before she met Prentice. She was not actively dating anyone, so  she decided to join a dating website and see what the possibilities were of meeting the right man.

While the chemistry was right between them from the beginning, they faced serious challenges. Maria was concerned about his sons because they did not want Prentice to remarry. They were very attached to their deceased mother. Prentice is considerably older than Maria, which created a whole new set of concerns. Maria spoke English, but not well. How would she adjust to life in the States? They did a lot of prayer and soul searching before they decided to move forward with their relationship.

While their issues and concerns did not magically disappear, Prentice and Maria believe that God has graced

their union. Since their marriage and Maria's emigration to America, both families have adjusted and accepted the reality that Prentice and Maria are truly in love with each other. There is a special place in Prentice's heart for Maria's mother back in the Philippines, and his sons have become much more accepting of Maria.

Prentice loves the fact that Maria is not overly materialistic and is satisfied with the good, but not opulent, lifestyle he provides. He is very appreciative of the way she takes care of him, her dedication to the marriage and to being his partner. Maria appreciates Prentice for the good, Christian man he is, and adores him for treating her with respect and tenderness.

When Prentice became a member of Christian Filipina, his focus was to find a wife with strong Christian values – that's exactly what he found in Maria. He has become a strong advocate of the website, advising Filipina singles to just be online, be available and be accessible so they can meet the person who is right for them (also, see a video interview with Prentice and Maria at www.globalfiance.com/testimonials.).

CHAPTER FOUR

Swimming with Sharks

I live in Hawaii, so I am literally surrounded by the blue Pacific Ocean. Without a doubt, I am blessed to have a home in paradise!

One of the more popular outdoor activities on the Big Island is snorkeling and scuba diving. As any experienced diver will tell you, there's always the chance you may run into a shark when you jump into the ocean. Is this a reason not to go swimming? No. If people made the decision not to go underwater because the sharks lived there, they would be denying themselves the incredible experience of floating weightless, surrounded by awe-inspiring beauty.

You just have to know a shark when you see one and what to do (and not to do) when you are in their presence.

The same goes for international online dating sites. If you're careful and wise, you can avoid being tricked into spending hundreds, even thousands, of dollars on sites that have no real interest in helping you find a soulmate. As you will see when you begin exploring online, many of these sites have one and only one agenda – to take as much money from you as quickly as they can before you get wise to their fraud.

Here is what a "shark site" looks like in the international online dating world:

If the site charges you per-minute, per-message or per-chat fees, they're a shark site. Legitimate online dating sites charge their members a flat monthly fee or at least have a rational, easy-to-understand fee structure that is inclusive of communications with other members. The sad truth is that many dating sites have become intoxicated by the profits generated by this "pay to communicate" method. Why do the shark sites do this and how can they get away with it?

Because…

The majority of the profiles on these pay-per-minute or pay-per-message shark sites are fraudulent. Many international dating sites post glamour-type cover shots of very attractive women to entice men to call and start a "relationship" with one of them. That's when the sharks begin to feed. Either directly or, more commonly, through an agency, the site employs professional models who are trained to not only show off their physical features, but also to hook men into believing that they are interested in pursuing a real relationship. These women – or in some cases men posing as women – pretend to fall in love at so much money per minute.

When the time comes for the man to fly to the woman's country and meet his fiancé, the women suddenly disappear. Sadly, many men repeat this cycle more than once, hoping against hope that the next time it will be different.

Based on my experience and on discussions with my many contacts in the international dating industry, I believe that fewer than 10% of women's profiles on these pay-per-message/pay –per-chat sites are actual, legitimate single women who are open to a relationship.

What I am telling you is not a secret, but the truth is that it is hard to find love among the millions of dollars of advertising, press releases and publicity by the shark sites. These shark sites openly prey on men who are sincere and want nothing more than to meet a foreign lady and fall in love. This is big business – the shark sites generate hundreds of millions of dollars in revenues annually.

Please do not take my word for it. Investigate this for yourself. Do your own Google search. While some of the largest shark sites spend millions of dollars trying to bury the truth, it's out there, in abundance. I offer several testimonials in written, video and audio form at www.globalfiance.com/sharksites where men tell their stories, unfiltered in their own words, on how they were abused by these pernicious practices – as well as from women who worked for these enterprises.

If you have fallen victim to a shark site and have not reported it to the government, please report it now. We have links, phone numbers and other contact information for the appropriate governmental agencies in the Appendix Resource at the end this book.

Recently I was interviewed by the *BBC* for their news piece entitled, *Tainted Love*. In this hard hitting report, *BBC* reporter Fiona Walker documented unethical practices used by some in the international online dating industry. I was the only online dating industry executive who appeared in the report. In the words of Ms. Walker, "Christian Filipina campaigns against bad practices in the industry." I was proud to help the *BBC* publicly expose the reprehensible conduct of the shark sites.

Here are some final thoughts to consider if you decide to investigate the large variety of sites online:

- If a real lady, a real person, is online looking for a partner, then she has real photos of herself doing real things – at social gatherings with friends, at church, at home in casual clothes, etc. Keep an eye out for posted photos of real people, not glamour shots taken by a professional photographer.
- If you search reviews of the site on the internet, do you find more good reviews than bad ones?
- Does the site take security seriously? It should provide you with general advice on how to be cautious of shark sites and individual scammers (more on this in the next chapter). All of the site's pages should be secured with SSL and should be certified PCI complaint.

- Is customer service easy to reach by phone? Are they interested in what you need, or are they pushy to make a sale?

It breaks my heart to hear story after story of Good Guys who became victims of the shark sites, in many cases never even knowing that they had been swindled. But with knowledge comes power. There is no need to go through the financial and emotional hardship that some men experience. Here are a few "anti-testimonials" we collected from the US government of what some men have gone through:

1. *"Yes, I have had a very bad experience. I spent a huge amount of money in order to exchange letters with a woman who was listed on a website from Russia. I exchanged emails with Ekaterina (Katya) for a few months and then made arrangements to fly to Russia to meet her. She had all of my flight information and knew all of the details about when I was coming so that she could meet me at the airport. She never showed up. She didn't even try to contact me at the hotel I was staying at. I freaked out on the web admin people and they promised to get in touch with her. After three days alone in Russia, I finally met Katya. I tried to talk to her but her English was not very good (her profile and her letters claimed that she was advanced and fluent). I asked her about things in her life that she had written in her letters...and she just looked at me...blank stare! It turns out that [WEBSITE] has a team of letter writers on staff who answer for the ladies. It is a pretty safe bet because most men who correspond with these women will NEVER EVER EVER put their *ss in an airplane seat and go visit these women. Needless to say, I was very upset and things did not work out with Katya, because she was not the woman who I was actually*

corresponding with. [WEBSITE] never never ever lets you have the personal contact information of the women, so you have no independent method of verifying the identity of the women."

Source: Internet Crime Complaint Center. Edited for grammar and presentation.

2. *"I subscribed to their international dating services to meet a lady from abroad and spent thousands of dollars in translation and phone charges for fake services. They have developed a nasty, un-permissive system where I contacted a lady by letter through a translator in Ukraine; the lady was supposed to read the letter and respond through the service of a translator. After 10 to 15 letters (at $8 per letter) the lady was accepting phone calls for $4.99 per minute (with a 10 minute minimum)...This is the reality: the translator was responding to my letters directly, the "ladies" did not even know about the correspondence, but they were aware of this practice. This agency was forcing translators to send "introduction letters" as if they were the real lady to generate income (for the web site) through letters and phone charges...When there was an attempt to meet in person she (the lady) vanished immediately. I was given a fake phone number, with no possibility to contact this lady anymore...One of the translators contacted me directly because she was extremely upset by this practice and saw I was too nice to be screwed that way. I am meeting with her in few days and she will reveal to me all the secrets of this agency, she is recording all docs necessary, I will interview her. They tried to oblige her to sign a special agreement to not reveal this forgery. This is outrageous! I have all docs proving this terrible, crooked business that left me dried and killed all my illusions of happiness. I met with dozens of*

Americans citizens who got caught in the same trap...my personal losses are about $10,000. I value my emotional distress to be WAY MORE. Thousands of people from all over the world are dried by these bastards. I want them in a court of justice and in jail!
Source: Internet Crime Complaint Center; amount: $10, 000. Edited for grammar and presentation.

3. *"I corresponded for 6 months with ladies from Odessa, Ukraine. I received 3 to 8 letters from ladies each day. To read a letter costs $8, to respond costs another $8. I travelled to Odessa to meet the ladies only to find they were almost all "on vacation" or "too busy" or "had a sick mom" or any of a half dozen other excuses. Their translators encouraged me to see the sights, as if I wanted to spend $4000 to see dirty buildings and rocky sea shores. Former translators for (WEBSITE) said they were paid $0.80 for each set of letters. To make more money the translators wrote LOTS of letters. The girls did not write the letters. At the most the translators telephoned the girls and read the letters to them, but most were simply made up. I did meet 4 of the dozen girls I had been writing. They were totally uninterested in anything but a free expensive dinner or gift, not at all the sincere women of the letters. When some of the girls left, they insisted I owed them for their taxi, from $50 to $70 (you can get anywhere in town for $6). I met 7 other men that had the same experience with (WEBSITE) as me.*
Source: Internet Crime Complaint Center; amount: $2,160. Edited for grammar and presentation.

The evil online cousin to the shark sites are the individual scammers. These nuisances are a plague to every international dating site, legitimate or otherwise. At Christian Filipina we take every possible step to identify and immediately ban scammers from our site, but our competitors are not always as diligent.

In order to have a successful online international dating experience, you need to know about both the sharks and the scammers…

CHAPTER FIVE

Avoiding the Scammers

It is a sad fact of life that certain people succumb to the temptation of stealing. Even worse, there are many people from every country in world who use people's desire to find true love as a convenient vehicle to commit theft. I find this behavior both appalling and sad. That said, scammers or fraudsters are an unfortunate fact of life in the international dating world. But just as with their evil cousin – the shark sites – a little knowledge and a few simple rules go a long way towards ensuring that you will not be a victim of their cons.

If I could tell you only one thing on this subject, it would be this:

Never send money to anyone you have not met personally, face-to-face. Not for any reason. If a scammer gets a hold of you and pulls on your heart strings, it might be very tempting to rationalize to yourself, "This person has to be for real. I like them. They just might be the one. I'm going to send them $50, $500, $5,000 or more, it's not a big deal …"

Do not be fooled. Almost without exception, if someone is asking you for money before you've met them in the flesh, it's a scam. Scammers are a serious problem. They cost people money and, worse, they take away people's hope. People join our site and other dating sites with the expectation that they might meet the person they have been searching for all of their adult lives, a true lifetime companion, someone to love. Scammers prey on that vulnerability. But keep your shield of wisdom ready. It's inappropriate and unacceptable for anyone to ask for money in a dating context, for any reason.

Another strong admonition to avoid getting taken:

Do not give your personal contact information out to anyone you have not corresponded with for at least several weeks. By personal contact information, I mean telephone numbers, email addresses, physical addresses, etc. In the wrong hands, this information can be used by criminals to defraud you.

Let me share with you some real world examples of scammers:

"I was new in using the net but should have read the warning. I was deceived and defrauded in a way of $3,503. Because I am a born-again Christian, I was too trusting to a woman claiming to be a Christian on her profile and thru email and phone. I don't regret helping, but the reasons I was told turned out to be all lies. She claimed to be a graduating nursing student with balance in school. Then she said she was an orphan and was raised by grandma, and suddenly her grandma was in the hospital so I felt sorry for her. In one month of xxxx I sent her that money thru Western Union. I caught her lying when I asked her the name of all the medicines she claimed to have paid for her grandma and she can't remember any, and yet a graduating nurse? I am a nurse myself so then I knew I was a victim of a scam... You can post my letter for others to learn from my experience."

From www.ChristianFilipina.com, posted on the "Research and Advice" section of our website. Edited for presentation.

"I was defrauded out of more than a couple thousand dollars. I never thought someone I was trying to help come to the U.S.

to work would ever deceive and betray me, but that's exactly what happened. She was very cunning. Well, a person lives and learns. Unfortunately, I thought I knew how to spot and handle a fraud, but I did not. I really got burned. I'm wiser now and know I must use all the tools available to make sure someone isn't a fraud. The really sad thing is I thought I was helping someone come to the U.S. to work on a 'work visa' they were obtaining and not as a girlfriend. My efforts to help someone backfired. This P... R... was/is part of a scam operation. Apparently she was living in General Santos City and finishing college in August when she initially emailed me. She claimed she had no family and was out of money. She said her mom abandoned her when she was 3 years old. After a few weeks she said she had been offered an "urgent hire" position as a caregiver at El Camino Hospital Foundation in California – which just happened to be in the same city where I lived. Then she claimed she needed to fly to Manila to "out process" with the caregiver agency who hired her. She claimed she needed money to fly to Manila from General Santos City. Then, when in Manila, she claimed to have gotten robbed and cut with a knife which gave her tetanus. Because of this she needed to spend a few days in the hospital…it goes on and on. The bottom line is she and her accomplices I... C...and N... T...all conspired to extract money from me through this elaborate hoax/fraud. Please inform your website subscribers."

From www.ChristianFilipina.com, posted on the "Research and Advice" section of our website. Edited for presentation.

"Oh my God, they got me for $2000 and $3000. She told me her mom died and didn't have any money to bury her mum. Then she said her mum had money but she can't get it because she needed it and she didn't have it so she gave me a check so I could cash it. I was so stupid, I put it in my bank account and

took $5000 dollars out of my account. She told me I can keep the other $2000. When I sent the money to her, she told me she loved me and can't wait to see me. Then my bank called me and told me the check I put in my account was a scam and I had to replace the money I took out. I was looking so stupid. The bank said it looked just like a real check, but many people had been scammed same way. So if someone tells you to cash a check for them run the other way. She had the nerve to write me again and ask me how I was and what did I do with the money from the check. I wanted to call her a whole lot of names but I didn't. I told her I wanted to come there to see her she had a nerve to tell me to send her some money to get her here. I told her to hold on and I called the police in Ghana. When I started back talking to her she knew something was wrong and said she had to go. The police told me they knew where she was chatting from. It's a place men and women work from to get money and they were doing this to people all around the world...Now I know better. It makes it hard for the honest girls that are really out there to find someone...

From www.ChristianFilipina.com, posted on the "Research and Advice" section of our website. Edited for presentation.

Forewarned is forearmed. I'm not sharing this information with you to discourage you from using an international dating web site – just the opposite. If you follow these very simple rules, you can avoid getting burned financially and hurt emotionally. At Christian Filipina, we work diligently every day to weed out fraudsters from our site. I know that some other international dating sites are also doing all they can to prevent fraud.

Shark sites, as discussed in Chapter 4, are generally not as scrupulous. So if you decide to use a shark site, be aware that you can potentially get burned both ways – by the site and by criminals freely operating on the site.

Alright, you know what you need to know. Let's get back to the reason why you are reading this book in the first place: to find your soulmate. While we cannot turn a blind eye to the problems in our industry, we also cannot discount the fact that Good Guys and Good Girls find each other every day and live happily ever after.

Folks like Michael and Lea McFadden.

CHAPTER SIX

Success!

Michael and Lea McFadden

Michael had never been married and Lea had been a widow since 1999. While an ocean and a cultural divide separated them, their faith brought them together. They are both thankful for the role Christian Filipina played in their romance, which culminated in their marriage in May of 2011.

Lea was working as an embroiderer in Saudi Arabia when she joined Christian Filipina in 2010. Her sister was also in Saudi Arabia working with her, and she introduced Lea to the website. After almost a decade of being single and living far away from home, Lea was ready for a new relationship. As a devout Baptist Christian, Lea wanted to meet a "Godly man" who shared her values and her faith. While living as an ex-patriot in the Middle East, Lea met several Filipino men over the years who were also there working, but she was often disappointed that their values were more secular than religious.

Michael was living in Arlington, Texas in 2010. After trying several other dating websites, he came across Christian Filipina and was immediately impressed. One key feature that Christian Filipina offered that the other sites did not was the ability to select ladies to correspond with who were Baptists. Finding a wife from his own denomination was important to Michael, so he began exchanging information with sixty-two women who classified themselves as Baptists on the site. Shortly thereafter, he met Lea.

While it took him a couple of months in Lea's words to "do the right thing", Michael began exclusively speaking to her on the website. Lea happened to have relatives who lived in East Texas, and Michael traveled

across state and met with them. This was a wonderful way for him to learn more about her and also for Lea's relatives to get to know Michael and share their impressions of him with her.

In May of 2011, Michael traveled to the Philippines and married Lea. He proposed and they planned the wedding before they met face-to-face. At their large and beautiful wedding ceremony, Michael was introduced to his new and very large extended family. They bought a house in the

Philippines to. Michael was very impressed by the Filipino culture and enjoyed being in a more conservative country where Christian values are more openly expressed.

They began the immigration process immediately after their wedding and in September of 2012 Lea arrived in America. The McFaddens now happily reside in Arlington. Lea has an extensive network of Philippine friends and family both in Texas and in Illinois. They are very much in love and have adjusted to their life together. Michael has developed a palate for Philippine food and Lea has learned to cook some traditional American fare. They both love their church, Trinity Baptist.

They also love Christian Filipina and highly recommend it for Christians seeking to find a soulmate overseas. (To see a video of them, go online and visit www.globalfiance.com/testimonials today.)

Randall & Anelyn Bergerud

How do you build a relationship over the internet when two people are thousands of miles apart? When you find your soulmate, anything is possible. You might even be able to design a house over the internet. As amazing at that sounds, that's exactly what Randall and Anelyn Bergerud accomplished.

Anelyn was thirty-two years old, from Tangub City in the Philippines. She was looking for true love and a committed Christian relationship. She had tried several online dating websites, but was unsuccessful in meeting the man of her dreams. One day, a friend told her "if you want to meet a serious, Christian guy" join Christian Filipina, so she did.

In just a few weeks, Anelyn connected with Randall, who

was living in Las Vegas, Nevada. "We began communicating and it felt good," Anelyn said. "I'm 5'2" and he is 6'2", but that didn't matter. I fell in love with him right away. He is a God-fearing man with all the right values. He is tall and I love his beard!"

Randall Bergerud, fifty-seven, said he felt safe on the Christian Filipina website. Everything about the website "just seemed right and made me feel confident that I would find my perfect Christian match." When he found Anelyn, he knew that she was the woman he wanted to marry.

They communicated for a while, built a relationship online and then Randall visited and spent time with Anelyn in the Philippines. They dated, fell deeply in love and got married in the Philippines, where they decided they would live and build a house.

Randall had to return to the United States to prepare for his move back to the Philippines. Over the next five months

they exchanged photos and designs via the internet and shared in the vision of what their new home could be. Their plan worked! By the time Randall moved to the Philippines, they had built a new home and they were able to start their life together. Randall and Anelyn have been happily married now for more than two years.

Anelyn believes that a truly Christian man loves you for who you are, is caring and shows their love for you every day.

"The sweetest words you can hear are I love you," Anelyn says, "and not a day goes by without Randall telling me how much he adores me" (For an audio interview, go online and visit www.globalfiance.com/testimonials today).

David and Mabel Morphette

The Philippines and Australia are separated by 3,600 miles of ocean and islands. They have different climates, different customs and a different way of life. For David Morphette, a missionary from Adelaide, Australia, he believed that his future soulmate was a Filipina woman who shared his Christian faith. But how do you find the lady of your dreams in another part of the world who believes as you do and wants the same things out of life? The answer for David was Christian Filipina.

For most of his adult life David, who is sixty-nine years  old, was a builder in Australia and operated his own construction company. In recent years, he began doing missionary work. He started traveling to the Philippines on a regular basis on educational and religious missions. David came across Christian Filipina in January of 2011, and immediately joined because, as he puts it, "You could tell the site believed in Christian values and had members who were honest and sincere."

It wasn't long after he joined that he connected with Marbella (Mabel) Rodriguez from Manila. "I was determined to find a beautiful heart and that's what I found with Mabel. We shared Christian values and I really feel that God brought us together," David testifies.

During a March 2011 trip, David met Mabel in person in Manila. Mabel, who is fifty-one years old, lost her husband several years ago and has three children. David met Mabel's family and friends and things immediately began to click. "We were holding hands a lot and I could tell that she was starting to feel the same way I was feeling," David says.

Mabel, who is a church leader, joined Christian Filipina for the same reason as David – she was looking to find a soulmate who shared her Christian values. When David presented her with an engagement ring, she said yes. They were married in June of 2011 in Manila.

"We are both very happy," David reports. "The Lord has given me a woman of God and we both love each other very much. God has joined us together as one." Although they married in the Philippines, David and Mabel are now living as husband and wife in Australia.

David offers these words of advice for others looking for committed, Christian online relationships, "Your chances of finding someone you can connect with on Christian Filipina are very good because, unlike other dating sites, Christian Filipina has sincere members who share Christian values and beliefs" (For an audio interview, go online and visit www.globalfiance.com/testimonials today).

CHAPTER SEVEN

Why Filipinas?

I never considered the possibility of dating or marrying an Asian woman until I found myself in the Philippines visiting the father of a high school classmate. My trip was not initially designed to find a wife; rather, I was exploring the country in my ongoing quest to decide where to call home. Yet soon after my arrival I was exchanging phone numbers casually and easily with beautiful Filipina ladies who were smiling at me on the street.

Soon I began to notice that most of the foreigners traveling to the Philippines or living in the Philippines were men. There was one main reason why they were traveling or living in the Philippines – the Filipina women.

What makes Filipina women so appealing to men from Western countries?

There are a lot of single Filipina women interested in marriage. The population of the Philippines is around one hundred million. Since there are larger families and more young people versus the West, there are likely as many single Filipina ladies in the Philippines as there are single women interested in marriage in the entire United States or Europe.

The language and culture of the Philippines is very familiar to Western men. There is a strong relationship between the Philippines and the West. The Philippines were a Spanish colony for hundreds of years. After Spanish rule ended, they spent nearly a century dominated by a relationship with the United States. English is one of the two main languages of the Philippines and is taught in school, so most Filipinas speak adequate English. Many Filipinas also speak two or more languages.

The vast majority of Filipina women grow up with a personal connection to Christianity, as the Spanish brought the Catholic faith to the Philippines. Today every Christian denomination is well represented in the country. Even if you or your eventual love is not a regular church-goer or Bible-reader, you will likely share common ground and be able to define yourselves in a relationship within a shared spiritual tradition.

Filipinas are dedicated to forming and providing for families. Because divorce is common in the West, many Western men are leery to enter into committed relationships with women from their own countries. In the Philippines, life-long marriage is still the expectation and goal. In fact, divorce is not permitted by Philippine law. The only recourse for a married couple to end a marriage is called annulment, which is a complex, expensive and uncertain process based on proving the invalidity of the original marriage.

Filipinas tend to be conservative in entering romantic relationships. At Christian Filipina, our surveys show that over 75% of the Filipina women respondents have kissed two or fewer people (17% of those responding indicated they had never been kissed and 60% said they had only kissed one or two people). In the Filipino culture, a woman who has had even *minimal experience* with men is considered to be less desirable. On the other hand, for a Western man, an attractive woman who has only been intimate with one or two men would typically be considered a rare find.

Filipinas seek men who are faithful, calm, hard-working and thoughtful.

In our recent survey, *faithful*, *calm*, *hard-working* and *thoughtful* were noted as very important qualities by over 60% of the respondents. In contrast, less than 20% of the respondents said that *wealthy*, *ambitious* or *physically attractive* traits were very important in choosing a potential life partner. So you don't need to be a millionaire, movie star or fitness fanatic to attract a great Filipina lady. They are simply looking for a real person to build a committed, life-long relationship with.

Filipina women are open to living in a new place depending on the husband's established life or plans. In our survey, over 60% of Filipinas said it doesn't matter where the couple lives.

The low cost of living in the Philippines allows people to live well there on less money. Every year, thousands of foreign men visit the Philippines and settle there for good or go back home engaged, pack their things and return to live permanently in the Philippines. While this isn't the best choice for everyone, for many men moving to the Philippines, marrying a Filipina is like getting two for one because a family can often live on a smaller monthly budget than a single man previously spends alone in his home country.

Whether you are considering living in the Philippines or you're seeking a wife to live with you in your country, Filipina women should be on your short list of promising candidates.

Once you start the process of finding your Filipina soulmate, the hardest thing will not be finding anyone who is interested in you, but rather taking your time so that you can meet and get to know the right person. I recommend that you spend three to six months online to learn more and meet people before you go to the Philippines. Then take a trip of at least two weeks to visit the Philippines. During that two to four-week trip, you are highly likely to meet someone who is your true love and be well on your way to becoming a happy couple. After you have met in person, you can either make plans to move to her country or start the visa application process for her to move to yours. Depending on your country, the visa process could take a few months to a year to complete.

Take a minute to imagine the possibility – in about one year's time you could be living with your best friend, lover, soulmate, lifetime companion… *your spouse.*

Here is what to do next to create that future…

CHAPTER EIGHT

Getting to Know People the Right Way

You can buy your ticket to the Philippines and go there without knowing anyone in advance, without doing much research and just stay in a hotel or beach resort. You don't need to use an online dating site to meet someone – if you're a Western male and you make yourself visible in the Philippines, women will literally start flirting with you from the moment you arrive. Although I used an online dating site to meet some people, I ended up marrying a woman I met at a roadside eatery, not one of the women I met online.

That being said, there are some big advantages to using a legitimate online dating site that has sincere members. Using a quality dating site will allow you to:

Easily review far more potential candidates who are highly likely to be single and seeking a serious relationship.

Slowly get to know one or more people online before committing to the time and expense of a trip.

Connect with a community of men and women with similar interests to share opinions and experiences.

How do you choose a great site? I strongly recommend that you find and subscribe to *at least one* online dating site. Take a look around and try out the free levels of several sites before deciding to pay. You should choose sites that charge affordable, monthly fees in the range of $20-$50 per month and have a large subscriber base (at least 1,000 members logging in per day). You should choose sites that provide members with educational materials such as articles or videos to help you learn more. You should choose sites that have a testimonials section, preferably including at least some video testimonials. You should choose sites that do at least a rudimentary review of profiles to screen for sincere interest and respond quickly to any questions you have about the sincerity of any particular member.

You should also choose sites that offer webcam video/audio/text chat as part of their service package. You should choose sites that protect your browsing with a "secure" site certificate (most browsers display a green bar or padlock for secure sites). You should choose sites that have a forum community where you can interact freely with other members and while you are out there comparing sites, we recommend you also do a search of reviews of the site by actual past and present members to see what they have to say.

Unfortunately, most international dating sites fail to meet some or all of the basic criteria I have just laid out. Why? It takes a lot of time and effort for a site to develop these features and these features often make it more difficult to earn subscription revenue short term.

Most sites work well on both desktop computers and on digital phones or tablets. If you often use a phone or tablet to access the internet, you should to test the site interface before paying to make sure that it is convenient to use with your mobile devices.

Once you find a reputable dating site, you need to create a personal profile. If you are not sure of the integrity of the site, I recommend that you set up a new email address and then register using your temporary address. After you register, write a short description of yourself and describe your reasons for joining the site.

The key to creating a great personal profile is simple: be honest. Be prepared to upload a few digital photos of yourself. Your face and body should be clear in the pictures. It is not necessary to get professionally taken photos, but you can do so if you do not have any good quality digital pictures available.

Keep in mind your desired lifestyle and values. While a woman's age and race may not need to match yours, your desired lifestyle and values should match. Write down some notes for yourself concerning your desired lifestyle and values, and either add these to your profile or use them as criteria to evaluate each person you meet.

I recommend you take some time to think about how important it is that your match has the same denomination as you. If you are Catholic, do you want your partner who follows the same faith? What if you are Born-Again? Or Latter-Day Saints? If you are looking for a lady of the same faith, be careful not to assume that because a particular denomination has the same name, that it is exactly the same

A church in the Philippines known as Iglesia ni Cristo (literally translated as the "Church of Christ") requires that only people who become members can find true salvation and be accepted by the church. For this reason, if you are not yet a member but your potential soulmate is, there could be challenges in marrying her. This practice of exclusivity is quite different from Catholicism, as the Catholic Church generally welcomes anyone who seeks to connect with God and his own heart.

Some people believe that the Iglesia ni Cristo has other beliefs that are so different from mainstream Christianity that no matter how high your tolerance level, you won't be able to sustain a marriage if one partner is in the church and the other is not.

While there are some completely free international dating sites out there, I believe that the value offered by legitimate paid sites is well worth the membership fees. Most sites offer a lower monthly rate if three, six or twelve months are paid in advance. Prepay to take advantage of these reduced monthly rates. Different sites also offer different renewal packages. On some sites the full membership charge will auto-renew. On other sites, a discounted or monthly fee will be charged on an ongoing basis if you do not cancel. If you are not comfortable with the renewal system of a site, you should call them and ask if there are alternate arrangements such as disabling the renewal option or paying via Western Union.

You can usually start searching for members as soon as you sign up with a site. You will be able to search by age, marital status and many more criteria. Many sites enable you to create custom searches so that when you return to the site, you can easily find new members who meet your criteria using your saved search. You can also save any favorite profiles to review in more detail in the future.

Hundreds of new ladies join a legitimate international dating site every day. Over the course of your membership, you should login daily to review the latest new profiles. Be the first to send a friendly message welcoming them to the site. All it takes is one or two sentences, such as, *"Hi, I noticed you joined recently. Welcome to the site,"* or, *"I noticed your profile was added recently. I want to introduce myself. Please take a look at my profile. Maybe we can get to know each other."* The truth is it doesn't matter what you say in your first short message, as long as you are respectful and friendly.

Some members will write back, while some will not. Correspond frequently to allow friendships to develop. Don't form expectations and try to keep your mind in first gear for a while. Get to know some new friends and learn about their different and interesting country and culture.

A good site will offer video, audio and text chat capability within the site. This is preferable to sharing your social media, email or phone contact information. When you use the chat features, you will be able to see and hear the other person. If she says her computer does not have a webcam, she may need to find a different computer to use from time to time so that you can see her. The same goes for you. You should also have a webcam working on your computer, so that she will be able to see you when you use this chat feature. *If she refuses to show her face for any reason or refuses to show her hands typing, that is a seriously bad sign. You should make sure that you see her face and hands typing, with the webcam.*

While it is good to mention that you are open to a serious relationship with the right person, it is also smart to be clear with yourself and others that you are not going to quickly jump into any kind of exclusive relationship, either online or offline. I recommend that you correspond with several ladies as friends first and plan to meet them separately in person on your first trip to the Philippines. *The only way this will work is if you keep your communication friendly. If you start to wax romantic online, you will end up making it difficult to meet other people as friends.*

Either approach is valid – to develop a relationship with one person or to meet several people as friends, although I highly recommend the latter. But you should not combine these strategies and try and engage several women as romantic interests. If you do this, you will very likely come across as being insincere, and your chances of finding a soulmate online will go way down until you change your strategy.

While I covered the danger of scammers in Chapter Five, some information bears repeating here:

Keep your conversations within the site for a minimum of several weeks. Do not share your contact details right away. If someone requests that you correspond with them outside the site, don't do it. Insist that you have a firm rule to correspond *inside* the site. This rule alone will eliminate nearly all insincere people who might want to scam you, because scammers have exactly the opposite rule – they insist on corresponding *outside* the site, so that it is harder for site management to detect their nefarious activities.

If you do at some point receive a request to send them money or to send money to any third party (package office, visa processor, job application fees, advance for an inheritance, hospital expenses, tuition expenses, etc.), simply refuse and report them to the site management. ***It is inappropriate and unacceptable for any person to request money in a dating context from a friend or romantic interest.*** Anyone who asks you for money or expensive gifts like this is a scammer.

At Christian Filipina, we are so firm on this rule that we even prohibit people from sending unsolicited gifts. If we find that any member has requested a gift or sent an unsolicited gift, we will suspend that person from the site.

I'd like to take a few minutes and introduce you to our website, Christian Filipina. I humbly believe that if you are sincerely seeking a Filipina soulmate, we are a great option for helping you make your dreams come true.

CHAPTER NINE

Christian Filipina

You have many options in the international online dating marketplace. While I have provided you with some rock-solid criteria for evaluating websites, I haven't had a chance to tell you in detail about what we do and how we do it.

Before I begin, you should know that Christian Filipina may or may not be the right site for you. In the online dating world, one size most definitely does not fit all. I am very proud of what we have accomplished at Christian Filipina, but that does not mean that every man seeking a relationship with a Filipina woman should automatically select us as their dating site or one of their dating sites.

We are all about sincere, Good Guys finding Good Girls for long-term, permanent relationships. While you do not need to be a Christian to be a member of and benefit from our site, you should be aware that the vast majority of our members are Christians and their faith is an important part of who they are. Our members come from literally all types of Christian denominations – we are by no means a Baptist, Lutheran, Evangelical or Catholic website. You can use denomination as a filter in your search criteria on our site, so if it is important to you to meet a United Methodist lady, you can correspond only with United Methodists if you so desire.

Regarding any dating website, the best reviews come from current and past members. While not everyone who has been a member of Christian Filipina sings our praises, I am constantly humbled by the comments posted by many of our members. Here is a sampling of recent messages:

> *"Your website is excellent, both technically and for facilitating communication between two people searching for each other. I have met a sincere Filipina and I have just returned from visiting her and her family in Pampanga."*
> From Robert, 65, Australia. Posted on www.ChristianFilipina.com testimonials section.

> *"Greetings in the name of our lord Jesus Christ! I just want to thank God for granting my longtime prayer to have a partner in life in his way. And to my sweetheart thank you very much for loving me and see you in August for our engagement. Thanks too to Christian Filipina because of this website I found my true love. God bless your website."*
> From Michelle, 32, Philippines. Posted on www.ChristianFilipina.com testimonials section.

> *"I want to say thank you for having this dating site. The love and dream that I have been wishing for years to come true has finally happened by the grace of God and the creation of Christian Filipina dating website. Thank you so much!"*
> From Randy, Tennessee, USA. Posted on www.ChristianFilipina.com testimonials section.

> *"I have found my future spouse. I hope you will succeed in your quest also. I still wish to chat to meet new friends and to inquire about the problems of your country. I hope to work there come late September as I am a social worker who wishes to solve such problems and to improve the way of life and work towards social justice and equality."*

From Keven, 49, Ontario, Canada. Posted on www.ChristianFilipina.com testimonials section.

I invite you to log on to ChrisitianFilipina.com at your convenience and review all of our testimonials. Also, please Google our site and read any comments posted online about us or about me. At Christian Filipina we do not shy away from the bright light of legitimate scrutiny and feedback and we do everything possible to help our members online experience be the best it can possibly be.

Christian Filipina is the first site we built and is our crown jewel. We have spent five years learning about this business, building out the technology and community and training staff. For an affordable, flat monthly fee, we offer superb customer service, a large membership base, the only fully secure international dating site (using extended security SSL), a library of articles and videos and even a user forum. We screen new member applications for sincere intent.

Our methods work. Thousands of sincere men and women have already met their soulmates at Christian Filipina. We also offer a unique *Membership Discount Program*. As an upgraded member at Christian Filipina, you will also receive a 10% or higher discount for a variety of services, including hotels and visa processors. These discounts alone will more than cover the cost of your annual membership.

Dream Filipina is a new service that we now have in development. While many members are happy with the inexpensive, self-service approach we have at Christian Filipina, we provide a more personalized approach through Dream Filipina, including additional in-depth recorded and live interviews, as well as group and personal coaching. Visit DreamFilipina.com if you would like to pay more for a personalized service provided by the same reputable organization as Christian Filipina.

Global Fiancé is the network of resources we are beginning to envision now. These may include other international sites, as well as visa processing, tours and in-country investigations of candidates. Visit www.globalfiance.com for more details.

Okay, so you've chosen a web site, gotten to know several women online, taken your time and now you are ready to fly to the Philippines and meet the lady of your dreams. So how does all of this work?

Read on...

CHAPTER TEN

Visiting the Philippines

The Philippines is an easy, safe and fun country to visit. Even if you don't have the best chance of meeting your soulmate, it is still well worth the trip. Known as the Pearl of the Orient Seas, the Philippines is home to a diverse population of about 100 million people who speak over twenty languages. There are cities, towns, mountains and beaches on most of the 7,000+ islands.

How to Get There

The Philippines has several international airports which are located in Cebu, Clark, Davao, General Santos, Iloilo, Kalibo, Laoag, Manila, Puerto Princesa and Zamboanga. The two largest ones are in Manila and Cebu. Manila's Ninoy Aquino International Airport (NAIA) has several confusing terminals. If you have a transfer planned in this airport, leave yourself an extra hour to find your way to your next flight. Terminals 1, 2 and 3 along Ninoy Aquino Avenue in Pasay City, Metro Manila act as the main gateway to the world because they serve more than thirty airlines flying to different cities around the world.

Cebu's Mactan International Airport (MCIA) in Lapu-Lapu City on Panay Island handles regular flights from Hong Kong, Japan, Korea, Singapore, Malaysia, Doha and China as well as chartered flights from the United States and other major travel capitals. The Diosdado Macapagal International Airport (DMIA) at the Clark Special Economic Zone in Angeles City, Pampanga currently services low-cost or budget airlines and chartered flights while the Subic Bay International Airport in Olongapo City caters to both chartered and cargo planes. Laoag International Airport in Ilocos Norte services flights from Taiwan, Hong Kong and Macau. Davao International Airport (also known as Francisco Bangoy International Airport) in Barangay Buhangin, Davao City handles flights from Singapore and other chartered flights.

There are two major airlines operating out of the Philippines. Philippine Airlines (PAL) is the country's flag carrier and flies to and from fourteen cities in eight countries. Their website is www.philippineairlines.com. Cebu Pacific Air, also a flag carrier, is known for its budget flights and frequent seat sales (buy your tickets several weeks in advance for great prices). Their website is www.cebupacificair.com.

One odd note to remember – there is an airport fee for international departures of approximately $20 or 750 peso of Philippine money. This generally needs to be paid in cash because for some reason it is not included in the ticket prices. The airport fees for domestic flights of around $5 are usually included in the price of your ticket.

Documents You Will Need – A passport and Return Flight Ticket

You will need to have a passport to enter the Philippines. In most cases, that's all you will need because citizens of the United States, Canada, Australia, New Zealand and most European countries will be given a 21-day extendable visa at the airport upon arrival. If you don't already have one, it is wise to plan ahead for your trip by ordering your passport six to eight weeks in advance of your planned departure date.

In addition to your passport, the other thing that will be checked upon arrival in the Philippines is to verify that you have a return (or onward) flight ticket to leave the country. While this requirement may not seem logical, you will not be able to get around it unless you are already married to a Filipina and you are with her.

If you wish to stay longer than twenty-one days, don't worry. It is easy to do so by requesting an extension and paying the associated fee. Head to the local immigration office in any major Philippines city at least five days before the date stamped in your visa and they will take your money and give you another two months. You can do this up to six times. If you do stay one full year, you have to leave and come back. Like the return ticket requirement this cannot be avoided by arguing or reasoning, so plan for a short trip to Thailand, Hong Kong or Singapore once a year if you want to live full-time in the Philippines without getting residency.

Weather and Seasons

Most of the Philippines is quite hot and humid for the majority of the year. You won't need cold-weather clothes unless you plan to visit one of the few mountainous regions.

The Philippines has two major seasonal periods: the "cold" rainy season (November to February) and the dry season (March to October). These are not always distinct, however. Good or bad weather can happen anytime. March through May are the peak or best months to visit, so this is when most tourists flock to the beaches and the prices of hotel accommodations can double or triple.

Safety

You should read the travel advisories from your country about travel to the Philippines concerning any safety or sanitation issues. Typically, I advise people to avoid travel to Mindanao, especially on their first trip, as some parts of Mindanao are dangerous. The rest of the country is remarkably safe.

Money

The Philippines has been experiencing a lift in its credit rating and general economic health. The peso (sometimes called piso) is worth about 2 cents US, so get used to carrying around high denomination bills (100 peso = about $2US). Most banks have ATM machines that work on the global ATM networks. Some are programmed to give money either in dollars or Philippine pesos. I always kept my money in a US checking account and used my ATM card to withdraw local pesos. Unless you have an obscure bank/ATM network, this method should work for you as well. I recommend making withdrawals of only about 5,000 pesos or at most 10,000 pesos ($250US) to avoid the risk of any theft or major loss. Robbery and theft are less common in the Philippines than in many developing countries, but I advise erring on the side of caution.

Transportation

You'll find counters for hotel transport and car rental services at all the airports just past the arrivals gates. Metered taxis are readily available at the international airports for transportation to the city proper or beyond. Hotel transport can be arranged with hotel representatives at designated counters at the arrival lobby of the airport. You can also ask people for help in using local transportation ("jeepneys" are cheap and noisy local buses). In metro Manila, there is a light rail system.

I don't recommend renting or buying a vehicle to drive while you're in the Philippines. It's typically easier to *rent a car with a driver* and avoid the stress. Ask your hotel if you would like help finding a car with a driver. You will be surprised how affordable it is, especially if you provide a detailed itinerary in advance.

Where to Stay

There are numerous hotels, lodges, inns and even temporary dwellings that are available for the foreign traveler. Choose your accommodations based on your budget and your desired level of comfort.

There are a number of five-star establishments throughout the country, but I've never stayed in any of them as I tend to be frugal when I travel. At Christian Filipina, we have negotiated discounted rates with hotels in many parts of the Philippines, exclusively for our upgraded members. The value of these discounts alone would cover the cost of your membership fee. You can also find other recommended hotels searching on your own on the internet or just ask around at the airport when you arrive.

Be Respectful

Many foreigners, including myself, fight the bad habit of pointing out every annoying thing we come across. As with all foreign travel remember that you are a guest in someone else's country. You are subject to their rules while you're visiting and you need to respect their ways and customs.

Making disrespectful comments about the food or local politics or how the Filipinas could do this or that better will not help you. While you might think it's charming to tell Filipinas how smart you are, behaving in this manner in public will make any Filipino around you begin to feel scared that you are out of control. The best thing to do when you believe that you've come across a custom or practice that is less than ideal is to write your opinion down on a piece of paper. Then stick the paper in your wallet. Bring it home and tuck it away in a file.

Practice common courtesy. Just because you come from a Western country does not mean that you know what's best for Filipinas. Humility goes a long way towards making friends.

There are many wonderful and many annoying things about every country in the world. Try to focus on the wonderful ones, mention them and don't dwell on the annoying things.

Fun Things to Do

You could plan a trip centered on scuba, snorkeling, shopping, beach walking, mall walking or even museums. My personal favorite is to visit farms. If you want to have a theme for your trip, do some extra research on that topic and then make plans to include those adventures. If you want to go with the flow and relax, you can plan to visit several different cities. Try out traveling by boat between Visayan Islands, try the local jeepneys or visit a few different malls. Just being there will be fun because of the wonderful people you will be able to meet.

Just Say Hi

If you want to meet someone, just go ahead and introduce yourself. Say your name and ask to exchange phone numbers. It's easy and fun to meet new people. As a foreigner, you will get a lot of attention and be given the benefit of the doubt by most people who will be excited to get to know you if you give them the chance.

Don't wait for people to introduce themselves to you because more often than not those people may have an ulterior motive. Take the initiative to say hello. The Filipino people will open up and show you their smile when you take a chance and just say hi.

Okay, so you're there. Now it's time to meet some of the people in person that you've met online. I can help you with this too. Following some simple rules will make your experience of meeting online friends face-to-face more enjoyable and less stressful.

CHAPTER ELEVEN

Meeting as Friends First

If you follow the method I've outlined for you, within the next year you will be on your way to the Philippines for the first time. You should have a short list of female friends you have met online with whom you have corresponded for a month or more. You'll have asked for and received their contact information, including cell phone numbers and email addresses. If you're lucky and/or have planned it well in advance, you might be able to meet several people without doing too much traveling.

Both Manila and Cebu (the two largest cities in the Philippines) have international airports. If you do decide to fly within the Philippines to meet two or more ladies on different islands, don't worry. The price is affordable, usually less than a hundred dollars each way.

I recommend that you stay in a comfortable hotel when you first arrive, perhaps in the $20-$50 per night range. Depending on the length of your stay and your budget, you may decide to move to a different hotel later in your trip. Once you buy a local SIM card for your phone (or even a new, local phone if you need to since they are cheap) you can begin to send some text messages to your friends to let them know that you have arrived and ask if they would like to meet you in person. ***Most of them will want to meet you.***

The most common and straightforward places to meet are shopping malls. If you wish to be more creative and meet at a park, restaurant or scenic attraction, that's okay too.

You should be clear in advance with each lady that you are looking forward to meeting her and that she can bring one or at most two family members or friends. Rarely will any Filipina woman ever agree to meet you alone while you are just getting to know each other – and I suggest you shouldn't try to fight this. I strongly recommend that you are firm that there is an upper limit of one or two people who can accompany her. If you ignore my advice, be prepared to greet three, five or even ten people, all eager to meet the foreigner who is visiting their friend or family member.

You should decide in advance whether you would like to treat them to a fruit shake, a meal or nothing at all. I suggest you make this part of your initial invitation. Here is an example of a text message that you might send in this situation: *"I'm in the Philippines at last and hoping to invite you and one or two of your family members out for a fruit shake"* or *"I'm adjusting to the hotel now that I'm finally here. Can you and a friend or family member meet me for lunch at the mall tomorrow?"*

When you are ready to go, put on some clean clothes and nice shoes. You don't need to dress up in a suit, as it will probably be too hot. A clean, unwrinkled pair of pants, good shoes and an ironed short-sleeved shirt will do just fine. If you have your own style, go with it. But don't wear dirty or worn-out clothes, as your friend might have a hard time explaining to her family why you were able to afford to spend a thousand dollars on a plane ticket but couldn't spend twenty dollars to wear decent clothes to meet someone new and potentially important.

When you finally meet in person, be prepared to say some nice things to your friend and her friends and family members. Try to ask simple questions to get started: ask about her day, her favorite places in her city, whether she has ever been to other places in the Philippines or outside the Philippines, etc. Be prepared for the possibility that she will be very shy during your first meeting, but don't assume that this is a sign she doesn't like you. Most Filipina ladies are shy, and it can take some time (even meeting another day later in the week) before she begins to open up to you. Take your time and enjoy the process of getting to know her in person.

There is no need to have a detailed interview at this early stage, although it is good to ask some questions to gauge her desired lifestyle and values and to verify whether what you learned about her online is true. If she says she likes farming, what does she like to plant? If she says she is Christian, ask her if she has a favorite story from church. Ask about her education and whether she enjoys learning, and what subjects she enjoys learning most. And ask her to teach you a few words in her language.

An hour or two is a good length of time for this first meeting. If you already know you want to see her again, tell her so. If you are not sure, then you don't need to bring it up. Just wait to see how you feel about it later. You can offer to pay for jeepney fare for her friends and family back to their home if you wish; normally it would not be more than a few dollars.

Keep it casual and friendly and afterwards, and jot down a few notes of how you felt. You could even take notes while you are talking to them, if there is anything important you want to make sure that you don't forget. You could meet two or possibly more people per day this way if you don't have much time to spend in their country. When you're back at your hotel, if you are a member of an online forum you can post about what each day was like during your trip and ask others for feedback regarding your observations.

After meeting several people, it is very likely that you will find one lady who shares your values and desired lifestyle. You will want to spend more time with her to get to know her better. All you have to do is call her or send her another text message along the lines of, "*I enjoyed meeting you in person. Can we meet again?*" If you are already feeling that she might be the one, send something like, *"I have been thinking of you and want to see you again."* Don't worry too much about the exact wording. Just be honest and friendly.

When you meet again, if you sense that she might be the soulmate you've been searching for, you can tell her that in person, even if her friends are with her. You could say, *"I'm starting to feel something special when I am around you."* Don't forget to tell her that you think she is beautiful. You don't need to wait for a response from her or expect one or probe for her feelings. Continue talking about more casual things. If you tell her that you are starting to feel something special, then she will start to ask herself very serious questions about how she feels about you and what she is ready for. Most likely she will also start to feel something special too because you are a good, honest, real guy – just what she has been waiting for and dreaming of all her life.

You might need to meet her again the next day too. At some point, if you are both feeling the same about each other, you will be ready to take the next step and get to know her whole family on their own turf.

CHAPTER TWELVE

Meeting the Family

Whether you came to the Philippines already convinced that one person is your soulmate – or you came to that conclusion about someone during your trip – you will have the chance to meet your potential future extended family. It can be overwhelming, but try to relax and enjoy the experience.

You can bring a small gift if you wish, even something as simple as a flower or a kilo of lechon (roasted) pork or chicken to share. Don't bring an expensive gift, as this could confuse people and set inappropriate expectations.

If you are much younger than some of her elderly family members, you can show respect by raising the elder's hand to your forehead (the custom is called "pagmamano"). Those in her family who are much younger than you may reciprocate by putting their forehead to your hand. It is a sign of respect to one's elders.

If you've brought pictures from home, this is a great time to show them off. If you have children, be sure to show pictures. Your lady's family and parents will be hoping that you are a good person and that you would respect that your potential future wife is still part of their family. You should speak honestly to them and be friendly with everyone. Be patient so that you can talk with as many people as possible, if only for a few moments each. When you are courting her, you are courting her whole family. Although you might wish to sweep her off her feet and carry her away to be alone with her, trying to do so would backfire.

The Filipino culture is protective of its young ladies, and you have to win the support of her family and friends before she will be ready to fully commit to being with you. You cannot divide a Filipina from her family if they do not approve of you. Nor can you accept her but reject her family. You have to find something you respect about her family members, because if you cannot, you will likely not be able to find love or peace with her.

This doesn't mean that you need to accept her family living in your house or gradually milking you of your assets. You should be clear with her family that you can accept them forever *to a degree*, but that you also believe in forming a new family and you expect to have some level of privacy in your own home together.

I encourage you to court your special lady directly – always give her compliments and attention, while being friendly and slightly less attentive to the rest of her family.

When you are ready to take it to the next level and want to propose marriage to her – whether this is the first month you have met or later on if you choose to take your time – just ask to speak with her for a few minutes privately. ***Then just ask her.*** Speak from your heart. If you really don't know what to say, here's an idea, *"I love you. I am pleased and impressed with what I have learned about you. I want to be together with you forever. Please marry me."* Try to speak slowly and concentrate on how your body and head feels when you tell her. Watch how she responds; you may feel more comfortable holding her hand or give her a kiss.

Either she will clearly be ready and tell you yes, or she might still not know how she feels. If she hesitates just ask, *"May I ask you this again tomorrow?"* Then you both can return to her family and continue to talk with them casually. Keep your cool. Be friendly with the adults and kids. When it's time to go, ask if you could visit again the next day or meet some of them to do something fun elsewhere.

If she is not yet ready to answer you, then the next day take your time and have fun with everyone. You could bring another flower. At some point, ask if you could speak with her privately again for a few minutes. Take the time to tell her how you feel and assure her that you would like to spend the rest of your life with her, go to sleep next to her and wake up with her.

I do not think it is necessary to have an engagement ring in advance, but it is always romantic to give her a simple, inexpensive ring or other jewelry item as a gift. You may find that things are quite natural and you happily decide together that you are the perfect match. If this happens, talk to the rest of her family about your decision. In other cases – especially if she has had only little or no experience with men – it might mean that you have to be patient and go back quite a few more times to reassure her that you are serious. Try to be as patient and as romantic as you can if you find yourself in this situation.

When you are meeting ladies online as friends, ask casually, *"By the way, how many times do you think a man might have to profess his love to you before you accept him as your future husband? One time? Ten times?"* At least then you will know the ballpark number before you begin.

I would like to add a warning at this point. Beware of the common mistake of thinking that just because a relationship with a woman develops quickly that it was meant to be. If you meet someone and all of a sudden within twenty-four or forty-eight hours you have no clothes on, this is not necessarily a sign of a lifetime partnership.

Think about your values and your desired lifestyle and take your time to get to know someone. The attraction, affection, familiarity and comfort will come with time if it is meant to be.

Now you're engaged! Based on my experience and from listening to others tell me about their relationships, there are a few things you need to know about being married to a Filipina lady.

CHAPTER THIRTEEN

From Engaged to Married and Living Together

After your visit to the Philippines or within a few months of your first visit, there is a good chance that you will become engaged. You will have found your best friend and soulmate and have the blessing of her family and friends.

What happens NEXT?

The answer to that question depends on where you are from and where the two of you want to live together.

Though you probably already know, let me just take a minute and ask you – would you ever consider living in the Philippines?

The electricity, water and internet can be sporadic; the karaoke, pollution, monosodium glutamate-inspired cooking and humid heat took their toll on me. The police and justice systems (unofficially) don't protect foreigners or poor people as carefully as they do the Filipino elite.

While there are some downsides to living in the Philippines, there are many great things that are simply impossible to experience in many of our home countries: abundant beaches with warm water, inexpensive public transportation, Thai massage and fresh fruit (especially the mangoes). Unlike me, many men are able to successfully adjust to life in the Philippines. It is hard to know if living there is right for you without trying it. If you think the Philippines might be the best home for you and your new wife, I encourage you to live there for three to six months, if that's possible given your personal circumstances. The experience will serve you both well no matter where you eventually end up residing.

Most likely you already know where you want to live. And more often than not it's in your home country. Let's suppose that's the case for you.

Many countries, including the United States, offer both a fiancé visa and a spousal visa. Your country may only offer a spousal visa. In either case the process is similar, with the main difference being that with a fiancé visa you are engaged (but not married) whereas with a spousal visa you are already married. These visa process typically takes from three to twelve months to process and requires you to send in paperwork about you and your fiancé/wife, as well as documentation of your relationship (including recent photos together). Except in extraordinary circumstances, you must actually have met in person and have a recent picture together to qualify for an immigrant visa.

There are fees to pay – a thousand dollars or more just for the visa processing is typical. Add on a trip for your fiancé/wife to Manila for her final interview, plus a flight to your country and you are looking at more than two thousand dollars in total costs for the process.

You may choose to hire an immigration specialist to help you review and prepare your paperwork. Using a specialist is not required, but it can remove some of the headaches if you are not confident of your ability to file the forms on your own. This service could cost you anywhere from five hundred to several thousand dollars.

There is an income or asset requirement in many countries to ensure that you will be able to provide for your wife once she arrives in your country. If your combination of income (from your tax returns) and assets (bank accounts, home equity or real estate) is less than a minimum threshold, you are often permitted to have a co-sponsor from your family who will take joint responsibility. They will also be required to send in their income or assets statements to the immigration authorities.

I am not a lawyer, so none of what I say here constitutes legal advice – it is anecdotal wisdom based on my own experience and that of others in our network. You should consult the immigration information for your country and an immigration specialist for your country. At our website, we have negotiated discounts with several immigration specialists for our members who have an upgraded level membership at the time of their payment to the immigration specialist. You can also find many immigration specialists for your country by searching the internet.

Together at Last

The time will come when you and your wife will be able to live together. Depending on your age and desires, you may decide to have children.

If you have chosen to someone who shares your vision of a desired lifestyle and strong, wholesome values, then many happy days lay ahead!

Ask yourself the question:

"What is your desired lifestyle for you and your wife?"

I recommend that you think this question through carefully and plan AHEAD. The more thought you give to this process, the better the result will be from a financial, health and social standpoint.

No relationship is without its challenges. Every person, including you and your future wife, has some quirks. Everybody has a bad day sometimes. Everybody interprets things the wrong way or makes an incorrect assumption from time to time.

When there is tension, the most common reaction for a Filipina is to bottle up her emotions and thoughts. Many Western men are flummoxed by this trait. If this happens to you, go look up "tampo" on the internet and read on about this common characteristic for Filipinas.

It's not just you or her; it is part of a broader cultural pattern.

You don't need to fight it; in fact, it won't work particularly well if you do fight it. It really doesn't matter whether you made the mistake that triggered the reaction or she assumed that you did.

My best advice is to go for a walk or a drive or build something in your workshop. Just get out of each other's presence for a short while.

Then, after some time apart that day, invite her to do something FUN with you. If she refuses, try not to get upset. Sometimes, these episodes can last 2-3 days at worst. But, Filipinas are forgiving women.

She will come around and be hugging you and by your side again soon.

We are all imperfect human beings. Patience and kindness goes a long way towards solving these minor wounds before they fester and become a serious problem.

After the "tampo" passes and she starts looking at you warmly once again, make love to your wife and get back to living your happy life together.

If your wife relocates to your country to live with you, you should help her to find quality Filipino friends and other women in general to aid in her social adjustment. Filipinas are not accustomed to life without friends. She will be able to keep in touch with her friends and family at home via email, Skype and phone calls, but having friends *locally* will be invaluable to her happiness in her new surroundings.

Pay careful attention to the values and work ethic of those friends you help her meet. Are they faithful, happily married women or are they single? Are they more comfortable in church or in clubs and bars? Think about it. Your wife will emulate them so help her mingle with women of character and loyalty.

Have some fun together, learn together, explore together and work on your house together. Enjoy meals and each other's company. Continue to spend time with her and with your friends and family.

Get her out of the house as much as possible. Don't pen her in. Filipinas love to have fun and don't want to stay at home all the time. Whenever in doubt, get her to a bbq with a lot of friends, laughing and jokes.

That's the ticket!

CHAPTER FOURTEEN

Success!

Sam & Chris Essa

Chris prayed for God to bring her a loving and responsible husband. She considered herself to be a true Filipina with solid, Christian moral values. She lived a very simple life in Ozamis City. At only twenty-three, Chris was in no hurry to get married right away; she feared that she might marry the wrong man if she rushed into a relationship. She knew what she wanted out of life and was willing to wait patiently to find her soulmate.

Since Chris was not in a relationship, she decided to join the Christian Filipina community to get to know new people and possibly meet her true love. She was attracted to foreign men because of their looks. A month or so after Chris joined Christian Filipina, she received a message from an interesting gentleman. It was from Sam, a Canadian in his late forties and the father of two children. He had been a Christian Filipina member for a few months and had been taking his time getting to know several women.

Sam was not new to the online dating scene, but he understood that it was usually best to proceed slowly. He was certain that Christian Filipina was the right website for him to meet the perfect woman. His patience and confidence paid off. After three months of reviewing profiles, he came across Chris's profile. When he saw Chris' picture, he was instantly attracted to her. They started chatting regularly in February of 2012.

Chris began to feel that her week was not complete without an online conversation with Sam. She admits that she was not instantly attracted to him. Sam was older, but she did not care about the age gap. She said that Sam did not look his age.

It took persistence and consistency for Sam to win Chris' heart. He spent the time required online to get to know her well. They enjoyed each other's company and never felt any pressure to jump into a romantic relationship right away. Sam told Chris, "You are a good person and you deserve a good husband." Sam was right; Chris did deserve a good husband. They just didn't know yet that they were destined to be together, but their love story had begun.

After a few weeks of constant chat messaging, Sam finally asked Chris out. She was a bit surprised, but she agreed to go out with Sam on a Skype date. It was a date that they will never forget. They dated several more times through Skype until they knew that they wanted to take their relationship to the next level.

Later, Sam's marriage proposal was made through Skype too. When he popped the question Chris did not hesitate: she immediately said "yes". Some foreign men prefer to visit their fiancé and meet their family first before they plan a wedding. Sam took a different approach by proposing to Chris and planning their wedding through Skype. They did not want to wait any longer because they were sure that they were meant to be together forever.

Sam talked to Chris' siblings to let them know about

their wedding plans. Her parents were working in Malaysia at that time, but they gave their support to their daughter too. Chris prepared everything for the wedding – the menu, the invitations, the venue and more. Sam took care of all the wedding expenses. He made sure that Chris got the dream wedding she deserved.

In November of 2012, they met each other face-to-face for the first time. Chris traveled to Manila to see her future husband. Sam flew in from Winnipeg, Canada to tie the knot with his betrothed. December 16, 2012 was their big day. It was a Christian wedding at the Sanctuary Church in Ozamis City, Chris' hometown. They celebrated their love as Born Again Christians and received God's blessing on their marriage.

Sam has filed for his wife's spousal visa. They are waiting for a few more months before they can live together in Winnipeg, Canada.

Mark and Claire Strum

"Age does not matter." This general statement about romantic relationships draws a lot of critical attention not only in the Philippines, but in every country. For some people, large age differences are a barrier that simply cannot be overcome, but for Mark and Claire Sturm, age is truly just a number. Claire was in her twenties and Mark was in his sixties when they found each other at Christian Filipina.

Mark recalls how he met Claire, "I first saw Claire on Christian Filipina in July of 2011. I was distracted by other women before I paid much attention to Claire. I came back to the United States after an unhappy trip to the Philippines. I was talking with Peter about getting re-registered at his site and that's when I saw Claire's profile again."

Once they reconnected, Mark called Claire her on the phone and they chatted online on a regular basis. Claire wanted to be with Mark, but she was not sure at first if Mark was truly ready to commit. Claire has always been honest. When she is asked if there was an immediate connection when she met Mark, her answer was a big "no"! She liked Mark's personality from the beginning because he talked a lot and she learned much from his stories, but she never thought that Mark was serious about visiting her in General Santos City, a small city in Mindanao. Mindanao is not always a safe place for foreign visitors.

Mark proved that he was serious when he arrived at the General Santos City airport on December 8, 2011. They did

not waste any time. Claire's family embraced Mark immediately. Their wedding was originally planned to be celebrated at a Baptist church on Dec. 23rd, but they had to move it to the next day because there were some papers that had

not yet been signed. Mark recalls that the pastor reminded him several times that there was no divorce in the Philippines before he gave his final blessing to their marriage.

Claire decided to relocate and start a new life with Mark in the United States. She was frightened at first to leave her family, but she is a strong woman and she knew what she wanted – a family with Mark. On her way to America, Claire did not have enough money to pay for the airport travel tax. She had to pawn her wedding ring to pay for the taxi cab and the travel tax! There was simply no other option other than to leave the airport and go to the nearest pawnshop. She now has her ring back after a relative was kind enough to retrieve it for them.

Mark and Claire have a strong relationship as a married couple – they share the same religion and they have become each other's best friend. Respect and love are the foundation of their relationship. Mark is very grateful for his wife. He says, "I've gone through a couple of things that were pretty tough on me. Claire has been my buddy through it all. I got both a sweetheart and a best friend when I married her. If you

think that you can have better than that, I don't believe it. I don't wish for anything greater than the marriage that I have with her. She's a real blessing. It makes life okay when you get up in the morning because you know that it's another day spent with your best friend" (an audio interview is available at www.globalfiance.com/testimonials).

Doug and Angie Chappell

Doug Chappell was searching for love. He tried to find a wife in his native state of North Carolina, but the women he was introduced to never became more than friends. He also joined an American dating website and met wonderful people, but did not find his soulmate.

For a brief time, Doug dated a Filipina who lived in America. He was fascinated by how she talked and looked and he enjoyed learning about her country and life experiences. This relationship motivated Doug to search for his one and only in Southeast Asia and the Philippines. When he found Christian Filipina, he was impressed by the posted member testimonials and by the overall philosophy and practices of the website, so he became a member.

Doug is now happily married to Angie whom he visited for the first time in September 2012 in Cebu. He had travelled to the Philippines twice before. On his first trip, he enjoyed the province of Tarlac and the City of Bagiuo and also visited a lady there that he met online, but it did not work out. On his

second trip, he fell in love with Cebu, but not with the second woman he visited. Despite his lack of romantic success, Doug believes that his experiences on these first two trips helped him to make the right choices that eventually led him to meet his wife.

When he returned home from his second trip, Doug became active on Christian Filipina. He recalls how he found his wife: "I started searching your website and within a couple of weeks I met Angie, the woman I ended up marrying. After we read each other's profile, we both felt very strongly that we had found the person we had been searching and praying for. We started to email each other and within a couple of days we were Skyping. It's just one of those things that you count as a blessing because everything fell into place. We felt very comfortable with each other from the very beginning. We communicated daily, sometimes twice a day, for almost three months before I came back over and we met face-to-face."

Doug believes that because of the high quality of communication that he and Angie maintained in those first weeks online, they were able to develop the confidence that they knew each other well. "We felt very comfortable, as comfortable as two people can feel not having met face-to-face," Doug explains. "We both said, 'let's see what happens when we meet in person'. We hoped and prayed that our meeting would confirm our feelings towards each other. We believed that God was directing us. It also felt right to have her family present when we met." Their meeting could not have gone better and within a short time they were engaged. "We knew it was going to take quite a while to get Angie a visa," Doug recalls. "We both wanted her to move to the United States, but we chose to get married in the Philippines so her family could attend the ceremony. I've been back to visit her twice since our wedding because the visa process takes so long to complete."

The Chappells are not members of the same denomination. Angie is Catholic and Doug is Presbyterian, but this difference was never an issue in their relationship. Angie took Doug with her to Mass in Cebu and Doug shared video clips of his Sunday services back home so she could learn more about his church.

We recently learned that Doug and and Angie are living a beautiful, peaceful life and are deeply in love. They currently own a small B&B resort near 100 Islands National Park in the Philippines, where they enjoy hosting couples from all over the world. Cleary, the time they were forced to spend apart only strengthened their bond further, and they are looking forward to a lifetime of bliss together. You can check out their B&B at: Olanaphilippines.com.

CHAPTER FIFTEEN

Words of Encouragement

In the first chapter, I made you promise. I told you that "the information I will share with you in this book will help you chart a course toward being with the Good Girl you deserve." I hope you feel that I have kept my word.

I understand who you are, because I've walked your path. For whatever reason – and there are many because every man is unique – you have not yet found lasting true love. Some of you might have had little, if any, experience with women in the context of romantic relationships. Others are on the opposite end of that spectrum; you might have been married once, twice or even three times before and yet now you're alone.

Until now you might have thought that online international dating was a pipe dream, a joke or a complete scam. While you have to be wary and prudent, I believe that I have proven to you that searching for a wife abroad is definitely not an exercise in futility.

More than anything else, what I want to convey is that *you have options.*

Right now there is a great lady in the Philippines just dying to meet you. She does not care if you're a bit overweight or that you drive a ten-year-old Toyota or live in a modest home. What she wants, what she is dreaming of, is someone who will love her, honor her and protect her until death do you part.

Are you really looking for that, a woman who will appreciate your love and devotion, not stab you in the back or run for cover when things get tough, someone you can rely on and cherish with confidence until death do you part? It is not easy to find these women in America or Canada or Australia these days, although I'm certain they still exist in every culture, even in one as jaded and damaged as ours.

Have you had enough of lonely nights wishing that you were cuddling on the couch with a great lady and not staring at re-runs on TV and eating frozen dinners alone in your living room? Or maybe you are sick to death of the bar scene, all the foolish posturing and wasted breath of useless conversations about nothing? Perhaps you're just not up for another go at a marriage with someone from your own backyard and you want to try something different.

Our life is the sum total of our choices. I assure you that you have another option to consider when you are looking for a life partner.

It's been said that the definition of insanity is, "Doing the same thing over and over and hoping for a different result." I challenge you to try something new, because what you've been doing has not been working.

If you're serious about seeking a foreign wife it is going to take time, some money and a great deal of patience to find her and bring her home. But I have given you all the basic information you need to be successful in your quest.

In the end, who is responsible for our happiness? Can we really blame someone else if we are alone in this world without a good wife?

Take control of your destiny. Step out with confidence and faith. Be ready to work hard and enjoy the ride, even though it might get bumpy at times.

You can meet the woman of your dreams! You can be happy!

Now go for it!

Visit:

www.globalfiance.com

Go now if you want a clear set of steps and suggestions you can take right away to build the future you deserve!

Member Surveys — Filipina Women

Q1: Where would you prefer to live?

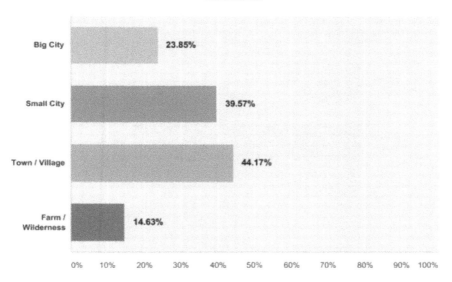

Answered: 369

Big City	23.85%
Small City	39.57%
Town / Village	44.17%
Farm / Wilderness	14.63%

0% 10% 20% 30% 40% 50% 60% 70% 80% 90% 100%

Q2: If you were to marry a person from another place, where would you prefer to live?

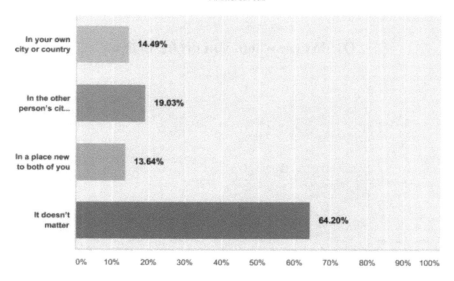

Q3: If you were to move and live anywhere, where would that be? Choose any that would apply:

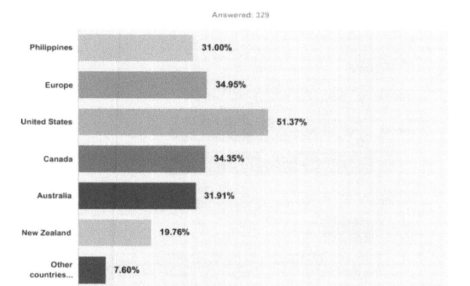

Answered: 329

Philippines	31.00%
Europe	34.95%
United States	51.37%
Canada	34.35%
Australia	31.91%
New Zealand	19.76%
Other countries...	7.60%

Q4: Which of these attributes are most important in a potential life partner?

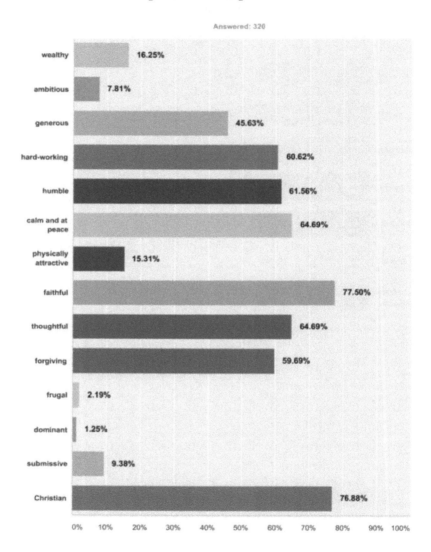

Q5: How long would you like to get to know a potential partner before marriage?

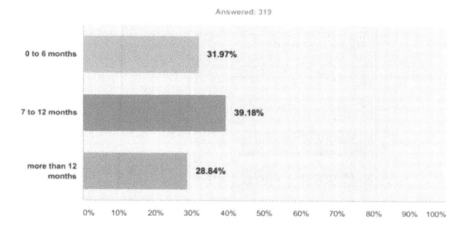

Q6: Which are most important to ensure a long-lasting marriage? (Choose any that apply)

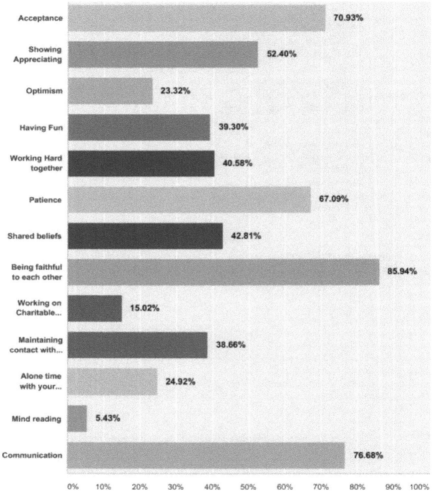

Answered: 313

Acceptance	70.93%
Showing Appreciating	52.40%
Optimism	23.32%
Having Fun	39.30%
Working Hard together	40.58%
Patience	67.09%
Shared beliefs	42.81%
Being faithful to each other	85.94%
Working on Charitable...	15.02%
Maintaining contact with...	38.66%
Alone time with your...	24.92%
Mind reading	5.43%
Communication	76.68%

Q7: Would you consider a relationship with a person that(s): (Choose all that apply)

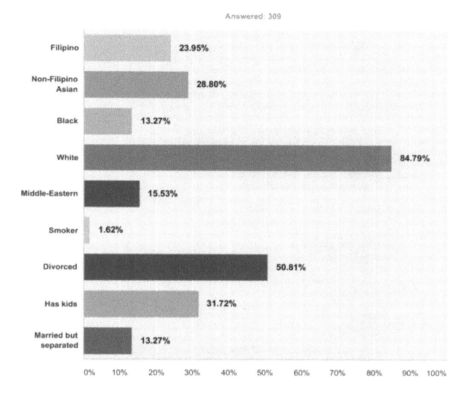

Answered: 309

Filipino	23.95%
Non-Filipino Asian	28.80%
Black	13.27%
White	84.79%
Middle-Eastern	15.53%
Smoker	1.62%
Divorced	50.81%
Has kids	31.72%
Married but separated	13.27%

Q8: What is your lifestyle? (Choose all that apply)

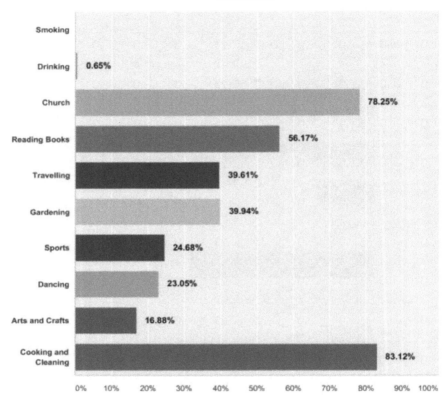

Q9: First date, where would you like to go?

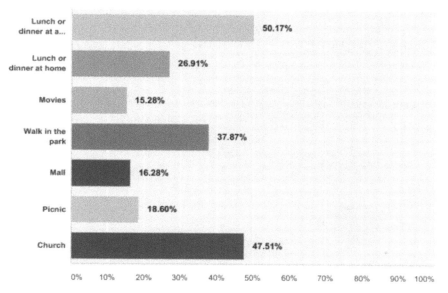

Answered: 301

Category	Percentage
Lunch or dinner at a...	50.17%
Lunch or dinner at home	26.91%
Movies	15.28%
Walk in the park	37.87%
Mall	16.28%
Picnic	18.60%
Church	47.51%

Q10: When was your first kiss?

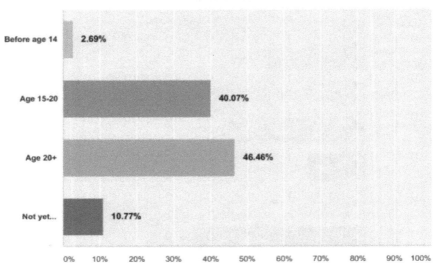

Answered: 297

Before age 14	2.69%
Age 15-20	40.07%
Age 20+	46.46%
Not yet...	10.77%

Q11: How many people have you been intimate with (kissing or more)?

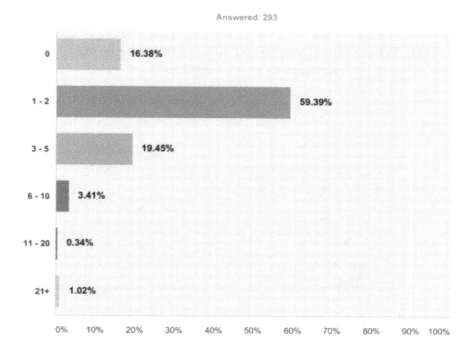

Member Surveys — Men

Q1: Where would you prefer to live? (Choose as many answers as you would like)?

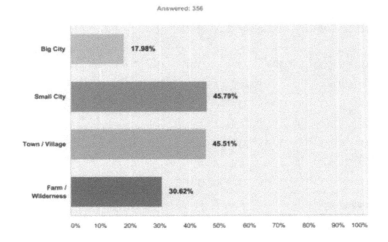

Answered: 356

Big City — 17.98%

Small City — 45.79%

Town / Village — 45.51%

Farm / Wilderness — 30.62%

Q2: If you were to marry a person from another place, where would you prefer to live? (Choose as many answers as you would like)

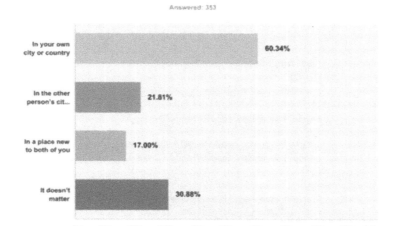

Answered: 353

In your own city or country	60.34%
In the other person's cit...	21.81%
In a place new to both of you	17.00%
It doesn't matter	30.88%

Q3: If you were able to live anywhere, where would that be? Choose any that would apply:

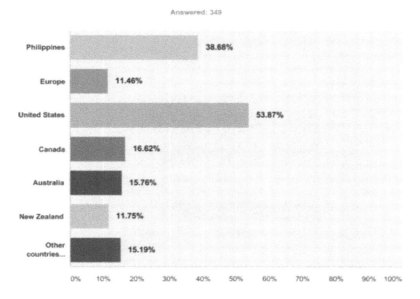

Answered: 349

Philippines	38.68%
Europe	11.46%
United States	53.87%
Canada	16.62%
Australia	15.76%
New Zealand	11.75%
Other countries...	15.19%

Q4: Which of these attributes are most important in a potential life partner? (Choose as many answers as you would like)

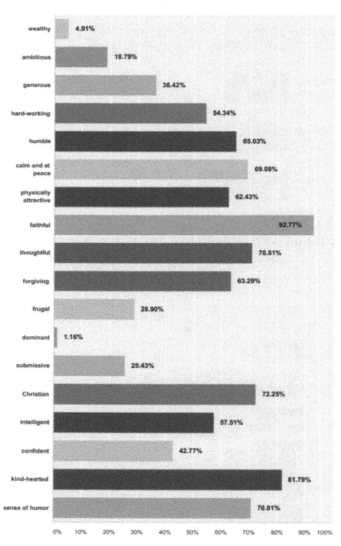

Answered: 346

Attribute	Percentage
wealthy	4.91%
ambitious	18.79%
generous	36.42%
hard-working	54.34%
humble	65.03%
calm and at peace	69.08%
physically attractive	62.43%
faithful	92.77%
thoughtful	70.81%
forgiving	63.29%
frugal	28.90%
dominant	1.16%
submissive	25.43%
Christian	72.25%
intelligent	57.51%
confident	42.77%
kind-hearted	81.79%
sense of humor	70.81%

Q5: How long would you like to get to know a potential partner before marriage?

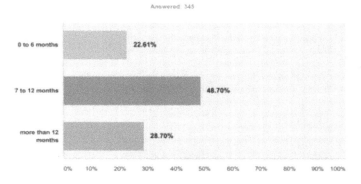

Q6: What kind of information/presentations would you like to have to help you marrying the Filipina of your dreams? (Check all that apply)

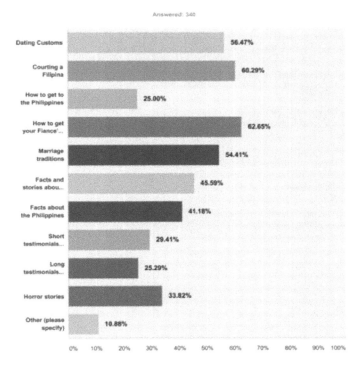

Q7: Which are most important to ensure a long-lasting marriage? (Choose any that apply)

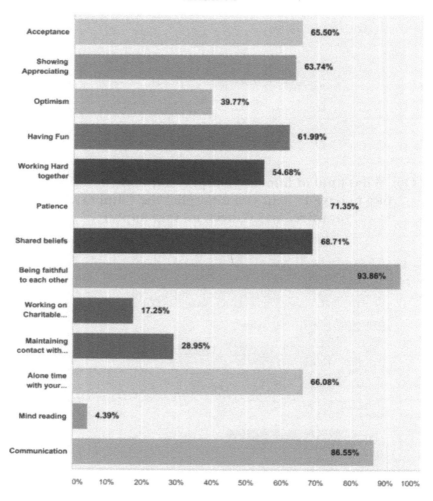

Answered: 342

Category	Percentage
Acceptance	65.50%
Showing Appreciating	63.74%
Optimism	39.77%
Having Fun	61.99%
Working Hard together	54.68%
Patience	71.35%
Shared beliefs	68.71%
Being faithful to each other	93.86%
Working on Charitable...	17.25%
Maintaining contact with...	28.95%
Alone time with your...	66.08%
Mind reading	4.39%
Communication	86.55%

Q8: Would you consider a relationship with a person that(s): (Choose all that apply)

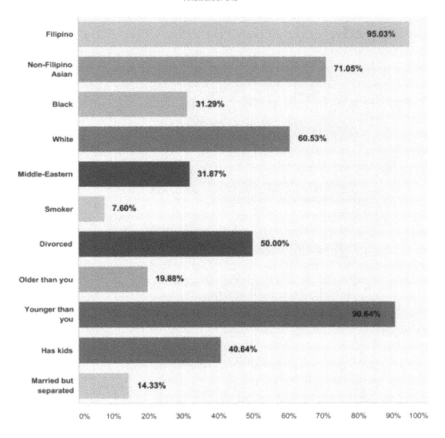

Answered: 342

Filipino	95.03%
Non-Filipino Asian	71.05%
Black	31.29%
White	60.53%
Middle-Eastern	31.87%
Smoker	7.60%
Divorced	50.00%
Older than you	19.88%
Younger than you	90.64%
Has kids	40.64%
Married but separated	14.33%

Q9: What is your lifestyle? (Choose all that apply)

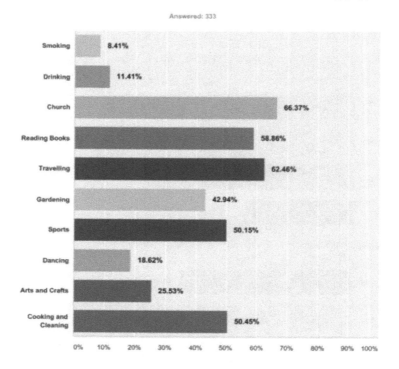

Q10: First date, where would you like to go?
(Choose as many answers as you would like)

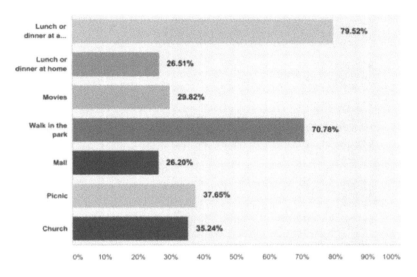

Q11: How many Filipinas have you talked / met so far through the website?

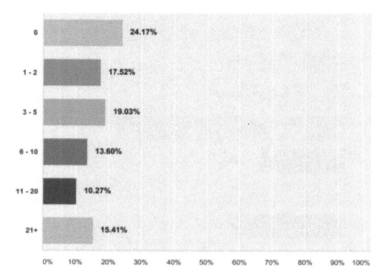

Q12: When was your first kiss?

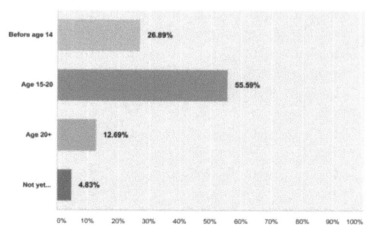

Q13: How many people have you been intimate with (kissing or more)?

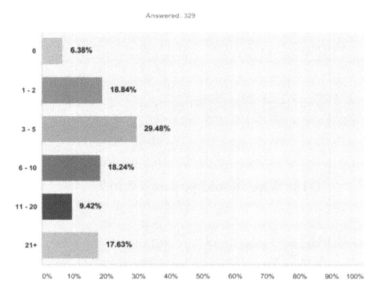

Q14: Would it be okay if your partner was friends with their exes on Facebook or on any social media?

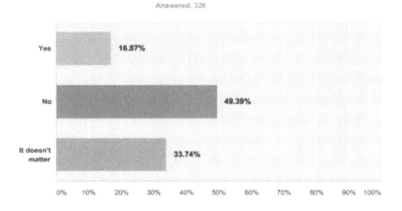

Q15: Are you friends with any of your exes?

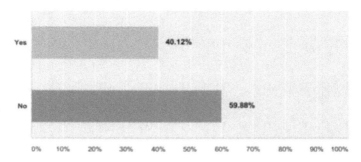

Q16: Who should pay on a date?

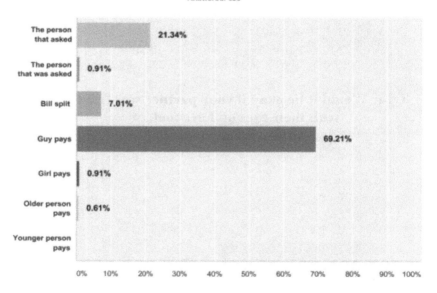

Appendix: Resources

A comprehensive, up-to-date list of websites, links and resources is also available for you at www.globalfiance.com/philippinesresources

RESOURCES WHILE ON YOUR TRIP

Philippine Immigration extensions can be obtained at:

AIRPORT OPERATIONS

Ninoy Aquino International Airport T-I, II, & III
Bureau of Immigration, Pasay City

SATELLITE OFFICES

Makati

BI MAKATI EXTENSION OFFICE
Board of Investment Bldg., Ground Floor, # 385 Gil Puyat
Avenue, Makati City
Pasay

BI PEZA EXTENSION OFFICE
PEZA Building Ground Floor., Corner San Luis St., Roxas
Boulevard, Pasay City

BI STA. ROSA Satellite Office
Brusmick Estates, Inc., Unit 2, 2nd Level,
Balibago Road corner RSBS Blvd. Sta. Rosa, Laguna
Rizal

BI TAYTAY RIZAL Satellite Office
Old Municipal Building, Taytay, Rizal

SM North Edsa
3rd Flr., Bldg. F, SM North Edsa, Quezon CityI TAYTAY
RIZAL Satellite Office

NORTERN LUZON

Aparri Field Office
2nd Floor Melval Bldg. RF Balizi St., Aparri, Cagayan

Tuguegarao Field Office
2nd Floor Public Market, Tuguegarao City, Cagayan

Dagupan Field Office
People's Astrodome, Tapuac District, Dagupan City
Laoag Field Office
Tupaz Avenue, Laoag City, Ilocos Norte

Baguio Field Office
Wagner Road corner Military Cut-Off, Baguio City 2600

San Fernando La Union District Office
Pennsylvenia Avenue, Poro Point, San Fernando City, La Union

Cauayan, Isabela Field Office
46 Burgos St., Cauayan City, Isabela

CENTRAL LUZON

Clark District Office
Office Suites Annex – Bldg.4B Birthaphil III, Clark Center,
Jose Abad Santos Avenue.,
Clark Freeport Zone (CFZ), Pampanga

One-Stop Shop Field Office
Clark Development Corp. Building 2127, Clark Special
Economic Zone, Pampanga
Diosdado Macapagal International Airport (DMIA)
Clark Freeport Zone (CFZ), Pampanga

Subic/Olongapo Field Office
7th 87 West Tapianac, Olongapo City
Subic Bay International Airport
SBMA, Subic Zambales

Bataan Field Office
Santiago Building, Balanga City, Bataan

SOUTHERN LUZON

Batangas District Office
Diversion Road, Barangay Bolbok, Batangas City

Boac Field Office
Boac, Marinduque 4900

Calapan Field Office
J. Luna St., Calapan City Oriental Mindoro

Lucena Field Office
2nd Flr. Quezon Provincial Capitol Bldg., Lucena City

Legaspi Field Office
3rd Floor, Velasco Bldg., Lapu-Lapu, Legaspi City

Puerto Princesa Field Office
2nd Flr. Servando Bldg. Rizal Avenue, Puerto Princesa City,
Palawan

Naga Field Office
Unit 7, 2nd Flr., Phonecian Bld., Panganiban Drive, Cor.
Isarog St. Naga City 4400

CENTRAL VISAYAS

Cebu District Office
P. Burgos St., Tribunal, Mandaue City
Mactan Cebu International Airport (MCIA)
Mactan, Cebu City

Dumaguete Field Office
Door # 8 Lu Pega Bldg. 38 Dr.V. Locsin St., Dumaguete City
6200

Bohol Field Office
2nd Floor Sarabia Co, Torralba Bldg., CPG Ave., Tagbilaran
City 6300

WESTERN VISAYAS

Iloilo District Office
Customs House Bldg. 2nd Flr., Aduana St., Iloilo City 5000

Boracay Field Office
Villa Camella, Boracay, Malay, Aklan

Kalibo Field Office
Municipal Bldg. Office, Kalibo, Aklan
Aklan International Airport (BIAIA)
Kalibo, Aklan

Bacolod Field Officeat the back of National Bureau of
Investigation Office, Bacolod City, Aguinaldo Street, Bacolod
City

EASTERN VISAYAS

Tacloban District Office
City Engr. Compound, Justice Romualdez St., Tacloban City 6500

Calbayog Field Office
Sports Complex, Brgy. Capoocan, Calbayog City

Catbalogan Field Office
#655 San Roque St. Catbalogan, Samar

NORTERN MINDANAO

Cagayan de Oro District Office
Door 7 Ground Floor, YMCA Building, Julio Pacana Street
Cagayan De Oro City 9000

Butuan/Masao Field Office
3rd Floor Rural Bank Bldg., A.D. Curato St., Corner PF
Lagnada St., Butuan City

Iligan Field Office
2nd Floor, Room 203, Diocesan Centrum Bldg., Salvador T.,
Lluch St., Iligan City 9200

Bislig Field Office
Tarefe Drive John Bosco, Mangagoy, Bislig City, Surigao del
Sur 8311

Ozamiz Field Office
3rd Floor Rizal Cor. Valconcha St., 7200 Ozamiz City

Surigao Field Office
Narciso St., Surigao City

SOUTHERN MINDANAO

Davao District Office
JP Laurel Avenue, Bajada, Davao City
Davao International Airport (BI DIA)
Davao City

Glan Sarangani Field Office
Ruiz Street, Poblacion, Glan Sarangani Province
General Santos Field Office
2nd Flr. Arcade II East Asia , Royal Hotel, National Highway,
General Santos City

Jolo Field Office
7400 Jolo, Sulu
Cotabato Field Office
Door 9, AI-Noor Complex Sinsuat Avenue, Cotabato City

Zamboanga Field Office
2nd Floor Radja Bldg.Gov. Camins Ave., Zamboanga City 7000

BORDER CROSSING STATION

Bongao Field Office
Ridjiki St., Bongao, Tawi-Tawi

Batuganding
Batuganding, Sarangani, Davao Del Sur

Tibanban
Orencia St., Bry. Tibanban, Gov. Generoso, Davao Oriental

BALABAC (PALAWAN)
C/O Elizabeth's Pensionne Tumandao St.
Poblacion II, Brooke's point, Palawan

TAGANAK IMMIGRATION FIELD OFFICE
Turtle Island, Tawi-Tawi
For the Field Office contact numbers please visit this link;
Bi-Subport Offices
-
http://immigration.gov.ph/index.php?option=com_content&task=view&id=128&Itemid=72

For Inquiries or other Immigration; visit the website; Bureau
of Immigration
- http://immigration.gov.ph/

Department of Foreign Affairs
2330 Roxas Boulevard, Pasay City or to any Philippine
Embassy or Consulate
Telephone numbers: +632-834-4854, +632- 834-3707 and
+632-834-4810

To Report Any Online Scam:

UNITED STATES

1. FTC Fraud Database -
http://www.consumerfraudreporting.org/FTCsearch.php

2. EConsumer.gov - econsumer.gov is a portal for you as a consumer to report complaints about online and related transactions with foreign companies
- http://www.econsumer.gov/english/

3. National Fraud Information Center - Fraud.org is a project of the National Consumers League (NCL), a nonprofit advocacy organization based in Washington, DC, was founded in 1899 to promote the interests of consumers and workers in the United States and abroad. Over its 113-year history, NCL staff have dedicated themselves to this mission through investigation, public interest advocacy and consumer education.
- http://www.fraud.org/

4. Better Business Bureau - The BBB Standards for Trust are a comprehensive set of best practices for how businesses should treat the public in a fair and honest manner. It's a non-government agency that handles consumer complaints against companies that violates consumer rights.
- http://www.bbb.org/us/

5. National Fraud Information Center / Internet Fraud Watch – Monitors different internet fraud crimes in the United States.
- http://www.fraud.org/scams/internet-fraud

6. Call for Action - Call For Action, Inc. (CFA) is an international, nonprofit network of consumer hotlines founded in 1963. The group's mission is to empower consumers by giving them a voice larger than their own. Volunteer professionals in offices around the world are trained to assist consumers through mediation and education to resolve problems with businesses, government agencies and other organizations. Our services are free and confidential and available to all individuals and small businesses.

- http://www.callforaction.org./

7. Nigeria – The 419 Coalition - The 419 Coalition is an electronically linked group of associates who fight the Nigerian Scam (419 Advance Fee Fraud). These days one could call it a form of Blog. Our associates consist approximately of 1/3 victims of the Scam, 1/3 of targets of the Scam and 1/3 interested in this matter for their own personal or professional reasons. There are about 50 active associates at any given time, though many others drift in and out as we address their needs.

- http://home.rica.net/alphae/419coal/

8. Internet Fraud Complaint Center - The Department of State's Bureau of Consular Affairsassists in cases of international parental child abduction. We place thehighest priority on the welfare of children who have been abducted across aninternational border. The Bureau's Office of Children's Issues is prepared toassist you in your efforts to return your abducted child to his or her countryof habitual residence.

- http://www.fbi.gov/scams-safety/fraud/internet_fraud

9. How to file a complaint - The IC3 accepts online Internet crime complaints from either the actual victim or

from a third party to the complainant. We can best process your complaint if we receive accurate and complete information from you.

- http://www.ic3.gov/default.aspx

PHILIPPINES

1. E-Mail Scam – How to avoid being scammed and where to report a scam incident.

- http://www.dti.gov.ph/dti/index.php?p=645

UNITED KINGDOM

1. National Fraud Authority - The National Fraud Authority (NFA) works with wider government, law enforcement, industry and voluntary/charity sectors to coordinate the fight against fraud in the UK.

- https://www.gov.uk/government/organisations/national-fraud-authority/about

2. Action Fraud - Action Fraud is the UK's national fraud and internet crime reporting centre. We provide a central point of contact for information about fraud and financially motivated internet crime. If you've been scammed, ripped off or conned, there is something you can do about it. Report fraud to us and receive a police crime reference number.

- http://www.actionfraud.police.uk/

3. Serious Fraud Office - The Serious Fraud Office is an independent government department, operating under the superintendence of the Attorney General. Its purpose is to protect society by investigating and, if appropriate, prosecuting those who commit serious or complex fraud,

bribery and corruption and pursuing them and others for the proceeds of their crime. It operates in line with its statutory purpose and policies.

- http://www.sfo.gov.uk/

CANADA

1. Canadian Anti-Fraud Centre - The Canadian Anti-Fraud Centre (CAFC) is the central agency in Canada that collects information and criminal intelligence on mass marketing fraud (telemarketing), advance fee fraud letters (e.g. West African), internet fraud and I.D theft complaints.

- http://www.antifraudcentre-centreantifraude.ca/english/home.html

AUSTRALIA

1. Australian Government Services Fraud Tip-off -The Australian Government Services Fraud Tip-off Line provides people with a place to report suspected fraud against Medicare, Centrelink and Child Support programs.

http://www.humanservices.gov.au/customer/information/fraud-and-security

2. Australian Crime Commission - The Australian Crime Commission (ACC) is established under the Australian Crime Commission Act 2002 as a statutory authority to combat serious and organised crime. We report directly to the Minister for Home Affairs and are part of the Attorney-General's portfolio.

- http://www.crimecommission.gov.au/organised-crime/fraud-and-financial-crime

3. Australian Competition Consumer Commission – Scam reports and complaints.

- http://australia.gov.au/service/scams-reports-and-complaints

4. Australian Federal Police –Internet Fraud and Scams

- http://www.afp.gov.au/policing/cybercrime/internet-fraud-and-scams.aspx

NEW ZEALAND

1. Department of Internal Affairs: Anti-Scam –Anti-Scam & Anti-Spam as reported to the Department's ElectronicMessaging Compliance Team.

- http://www.dia.govt.nz/Services-Anti-Spam-Reported-Scams

2. New Zealand Police: Anti-Spam Unit – Handles Internet Scams and Fraud.

- http://www.police.govt.nz/safety/internet.scams.html

EUROPIAN UNION

1. European Anti-Fraud Office –EU fraud investigative body.

- http://ec.europa.eu/anti_fraud/about-us/mission/index_en.htm

2. Europol – EC3 - Following a feasibility study conducted by Rand Corporation Europe, the European Commission decided to establish a European Cybercrime Centre (EC3) at Europol. The Centre will be the focal point in the EU's fight against cybercrime, contributing to faster reactions in the event of online crimes. It will support Member

States and the European Union's institutions in building operational and analytical capacity for investigations and cooperation with international partners.

- https://www.europol.europa.eu/ec3

JAPAN

1. Japan Company Trust Organization – Anti-fraud Organization in Japan.
- http://www.japancompanytrust.org/complaints/
2. National Police Agency – Japan's national police handles all internet related crimes or cybercrime.- http://www.npa.go.jp/english/index.htm

Country Specific Resources

United States

I. Travel Documents

As taken from http://travel.state.gov/. A service of the Bureau of Consular Affairs of the U.S. Department of State.

A. **Passports**
1. **Get or Renew Passports -**
http://travel.state.gov/passport/passport_1738.html
2. **Check Status of Your Application Online**
http://travel.state.gov/passport/status/status_2567.html
3. **Lost or Stolen Passport -**
http://travel.state.gov/passport/lost/lost_848.html
4. **Miscellaneous Passport concerns -**
http://travel.state.gov/index.html
B. **Visas (Foreign Citizens)**
1. **Visa Policy and Procedure -**
http://travel.state.gov/visa/visa_1750.html
2. **Business Visas -**
http://travel.state.gov/visa/temp/types/types_2664.html
3. **Visa Bulletins -**
http://travel.state.gov/visa/bulletin/bulletin_1770.html
4. **Visa Waiver Program -**
https://www.facebook.com/travelgov
C. **Visas (U.S. Citizens)**
1. **Visas for Entry Into Foreign Countries -**
http://travel.state.gov/travel/cis_pa_tw/cis/cis_4965.html

D. **More Travel Information**
   1. **Authentication of Documents** - In accordance with 22 CFR, Part 131, the Office of Authentications provides signed certificates of authenticity for a variety of documents to individuals, institutions and government agencies. Examples of documents that may require authentication for use abroad may include, but are not limited to, company bylaws, powers of attorney, trademarks, diplomas, treaties, warrants, extraditions, agreements, certificates of good standing and courier letters.
      - http://www.state.gov/m/a/auth/index.htm
   2. **Trusted Traveler Programs** - CBP's Trusted Traveler Programs provide expedited travel for pre-approved, low risk travelers through dedicated lanes and kiosks.
      - http://cbp.gov/xp/cgov/travel/trusted_traveler/
   3. **Join Consular Affairs on Facebook** - https://www.facebook.com/travelgov
   4. **Follow@TravelGov on Twitter** - https://twitter.com/travelgov

II. **Resources**

A. **Preparing for a Trip Abroad**
   1. **Sign Up for Email Travel Warnings** - The **Smart Traveler Enrollment Program** (STEP) is a free service provided by the U.S. Government to U.S. citizens who are traveling to or living in, a foreign country.

      STEP allows you to enter information about your upcoming trip abroad so that the Department of State can better assist you in an emergency.

STEP also allows Americans residing abroad to get routine information from the nearest U.S. embassy or consulate.

- https://step.state.gov/step/

2. **Read Current Travel Warnings** - Travel Warnings are issued when long-term, protracted conditions that make a country dangerous or unstable lead the State Department to recommend that Americans avoid or consider the risk of travel to that country. A Travel Warning is also issued when the U.S. Government's ability to assist American citizens is constrained due to the closure of an embassy or consulate or because of a d**rawdown of its staff.**

- http://travel.state.gov/travel/cis_pa_tw/tw/tw_1764.html

3. **Students Abroad Website** – Student's guide when travelling abroad.

-http://studentsabroad.state.gov/content/pdfs/Safety-v1.pdf

4. **Travel Tips for Everyone** – Quick tips on how to make your travel easier and safer.

- http://travel.state.gov/travel/tips/tips_1232.html

5. **Travel Tips for Older Americans** – Special planning tips for Older Americans.

6. **Beware of Scams** - International Financial Scams – Internet Dating, Inheritance, Work Permits, Overpayment and MoneyLaundering

- http://travel.state.gov/pdf/international_financial_scams_brochure.pdf

7. **Currency Exchange Rates -** Exchange Rates and International Data

- http://www.federalreserve.gov/econresdata/statisticsdata.htm

8. **A-Z List of Countries** – Country profile

- http://www.state.gov/misc/list/index.htm

9. **Other Travel Concerns** – Miscelaneous travel concerns and FAQs from the State Department
   - http://travel.state.gov/index.html

More U.S. Government Websites

1. **Center for Disease Control (CDC): Traveler's Health** - The CDC (Centers for Disease Control and Prevention) is an agency of the US federal government and is headquartered near Atlanta, Georgia. It focuses on the prevention of diseases and the promotion of health through research and through investigation of disease clusters and outbreaks.
   - http://wwwnc.cdc.gov/travel

2. **Customs and Border Protection: Returning to the U.S.** - All travelers – both visitors, Legal Permanent Residents and U.S. citizens – are subject to laws and inspections enforced and conducted by U.S. Customs and Border Protection.
   - http://www.cbp.gov/xp/cgov/travel/

3. **Transportation Security Administration** - Following September 11, 2001, the Transportation Security Administration (TSA) was created to strengthen the security of the nation's transportation systems and ensure the freedom of movement for people and commerce. Today, TSA secures the nation's airports and screens all commercial airline passengers and baggage. TSA uses a risk-based strategy and works closely with transportation, law enforcement and intelligence communities to set the standard for excellence in transportation security.
   - http://www.tsa.gov/traveler-information

4. **Animal and Plant Inspection** - The Animal and Plant Health Inspection Service is a multi-faceted Agency with a broad mission area that includes protecting and promoting U.S. agricultural health,

regulating genetically engineered organisms, administering the Animal Welfare Act and carrying out wildlife damage management activities. These efforts support the overall mission of USDA, which is to protect and promote food, agriculture, natural resources and related issues.

- http://www.aphis.usda.gov/

5. **Federal Trade Commission** - The FTC is the only federal agency with both consumer protection and competition jurisdiction in broad sectors of the economy. The FTC pursues vigorous and effective law enforcement; advances consumers' interests by sharing its expertise with federal and state legislatures and U.S. and international government agencies; develops policy and research tools through hearings, workshops and conferences; and creates practical and plain-language educational programs for consumers and businesses in a global marketplace with constantly changing technologies.

- http://www.consumerfraudreporting.org/cfr.php?URL=http%3A%2F%2Fwww.ftc.gov/

   a.   **FTC Fraud Database -** http://www.consumerfraudreporting.org/FTCsearch.php

6. **U.S. Postal Service -** https://www.usps.com/

7. **Secret Service -** The United States Secret Service safegua rds the nation's financial infrastructure and payment systems to preserve the integrity of the economy and to protect national leaders, visiting heads of state and government, designated sites and National Special Security Events.

- http://www.secretservice.gov/

8. **State Attorney General -** As the chief legal officer of the states, commonwealths and territories of the United States, the Attorneys General serve as counselors to their legislatures and state agencies

and also as the "People's Lawyer" for all citizens. Originating in the mid-13th century in the office of England's "King's Attorney," the office had become, by the American Revolution, one of advisor to the Crown and to government agencies. (Other resources http://www.naag.org/)

- http://www.consumerfraudreporting.org/stateattorn eygenerallist.php

9. **Securities and Exchange Commission** - The U.S. Securities and Exchange Commission protects investors, maintain fair orderly and efficient markets and facilitate capital formation.

    - http://www.sec.gov/

10. **International Consumer Protection and Enforcement Network**

    An organization composed of consumer protection authorities from over 50 countries, whose aim is to:
    - Protect consumers' economic interests around the world,
    - Share information about cross-border commercial activities that may affect consumer welfare,
    - Encourage global cooperation among law enforcement agencies.
        - https://icpen.org/

    a. **EConsumer.gov** - econsumer.gov is a portal for youas a consumer to report complaints about online and related transactions with foreign companies.

        - http://www.econsumer.gov/english/

B. **National Center for Health Statistics** - In the United States, vital records such as birth certificates, death certificates and frequently marriage certificates are maintained by the Office of Vital Statistics or Office of Vital Records in each individual state. Other documents such as deeds, mortgage documents, name change documents and divorce records, as well as marriage certificates for those states not centralizing these records, are maintained by the Clerk of Court of each individual county.

- http://www.cdc.gov/nchs/index.htm

   1. **Where to Write for Vital Records Per State**
      - http://www.cdc.gov/nchs/w2w.htm

C. **U.S. Non-government Anti-Fraud Agencies**

   1. **National Fraud Information Center** - Fraud.org is a project of the National Consumers League (NCL), a nonprofit advocacy organization based in Washington, DC, was founded in 1899 to promote the interests of consumers and workers in the United States and abroad. Over its 113-year history, NCL staff have dedicated themselves to this mission through investigation, public interest advocacy and consumer education.
      - http://www.fraud.org/

   2. **Better Business Bureau -** The BBB Standards for Trust are a comprehensive set of best practices for how businesses should treat the public in a fair and honest manner. It's a non-government agency that handles consumer complaints against companies that violates consumer rights.
      - http://www.bbb.org/us/

   3. **National Fraud Information Center / Internet Fraud Watch** – Monitors different internet fraud crimes in the United States.
      - http://www.fraud.org/scams/internet-fraud

   4. **Call for Action** - Call For Action, Inc. (CFA) is an international, nonprofit network of consumer hotlines founded in 1963. The group's mission is to empower consumers by giving them a voice larger than their own. Volunteer professionals in offices around the world are trained to assist consumers

through mediation and education to resolve problems with businesses, government agencies and other organizations. Our services are free and confidential and available to all individuals and small businesses.
- http://www.callforaction.org./

5. **Nigeria – The 419 Coalition** - The 419 Coalition is an electronically linked group of associates who fight the Nigerian Scam (419 Advance Fee Fraud). These days one could call it a form of Blog. Our associates consist approximately of 1/3 victims of the Scam, 1/3 of targets of the Scam and 1/3 interested in this matter for their own personal or professional reasons. There are about 50 active associates at any given time, though many others drift in and out as we address their needs.
- http://home.rica.net/alphae/419coal/

III. **Emergency Information**

As taken from http://travel.state.gov/. A service of the Bureau of Consular Affairs of the U.S. Department of State.

A. **For Americans Abroad**

1. **Crisis Situation -** What the Department of State Can and Can't Do in a Crisis
- http://www.travel.state.gov/travel/tips/emergencies/emergencies_1212.html

2. **Victims of Crime** - Help for American Victims of Crime Overseas
- http://www.travel.state.gov/travel/tips/emergencies/victims_crime_overseas/victims_crime_overseas_1748.html

3. **Financial Assistance** – Financial assistance for U.S. Citizens Abroad
- http://travel.state.gov/law/citizenship/citizenship_775.html

4. **Medical Emergencies -** Air Ambulance/MedEvac/Medical Escort Providers -http://travel.state.gov/travel/tips/emergencies/emer gencies_5981.html

5. **Lost or Stolen Passports** – Procedures on Lost or Stolen Passports - http://travel.state.gov/passport/lost/lost_848.html

B. **For Families in the U.S.**

1. **Hotline for American Travelers: 202-647-5225 -** Help for American Victims of Crime Overseas -http://travel.state.gov/travel/tips/emergencies/ victims_crime_overseas/victims_crime_overseas_17 48.html

2. **Injury or Death of an American Abroad -** Arrests/detentions/deAths/serious INJURIES OF FOREIGN NATIONALS - http://travel.state.gov/pdf/cna/CNA%20Standard% 20Operating%20Procedure.pdf

3. **Sending Money to U.S. Citizens Abroad** – Options and procedures when sending money abroad -http://travel.state.gov/travel/tips/emergencies/mone y/money_1224.html

4. **Welfare and Whereabouts inquiries** – Consular affairs FAQ sheet - http://travel.state.gov/pdf/ca_fact_sheet.pdf

C. **For Child Abduction Cases**

1. **Abduction in Progress** – Standard operating procedures in an actual event of an abduction - http://travel.state.gov/abduction/emergencies/emerge ncies_3845.html

2. **Assistance in Recovering an Abducted Child -** The Department of State's Bureau of Consular Affairs assists in cases of international parental child abduction. We place the highest priority on the welfare of children who have been abducted across an international border. The Bureau's Office of

Children's Issues is prepared to assist you in your efforts to return your abducted child to his or her country of habitual residence. - http://travel.state.gov/abduction/abduction_580.html

IV. **U.S. Immigration**

A. Citizenship – Citizenship Application and procedure
http://www.uscis.gov/portal/site/uscis/menuitem.eb1d
4c2a3e5b9ac89243c6a7543f6d1a/?vgnextoid=a2ec681
1264a3210VgnVCM100000b92ca60aRCRD&vgnextc
hannel=a2ec6811264a3210VgnVCM100000b92ca60a
RCRD

B. Green Card – All Green Card related concerns -
http://www.uscis.gov/portal/site/uscis/menuitem.eb1d
4c2a3e5b9ac89243c6a7543f6d1a/?vgnextoid=ae853a
d15c673210VgnVCM100000082ca60aRCRD&vgnex
tchannel=ae853ad15c673210VgnVCM100000082ca6
0aRCRD

C. Family Visa – Visa application and procedure
http://www.uscis.gov/portal/site/uscis/menuitem.eb1
d4c2a3e5b9ac89243c6a7543f6d1a/?vgnextoid=b72e
901bf9873210VgnVCM100000082ca60aRCRD&vg
nextchannel=b72e901bf9873210VgnVCM10000008
2ca60aRCRD

D. Popular Forms – USCIS Immigration Forms
http://www.uscis.gov/portal/site/uscis/menuitem.eb1
d4c2a3e5b9ac89243c6a7543f6d1a/?vgnextoid=db02
9c7755cb9010VgnVCM10000045f3d6a1RCRD&vg
nextchannel=db029c7755cb9010VgnVCM10000045
f3d6a1RCRD

V. **Federal Bureau of Investigation**

  A. **Official Website** - http://www.fbi.gov/
    1. **Contact Information -** http://www.fbi.gov/contact-us
    2. **Internet Fraud Complaint Center** - The Department of State's Bureau of Consular Affairs assists in cases of international parental child abduction. We place the highest priority on the welfare of children who have been abducted across an international border. The Bureau's Office of Children's Issues is prepared to assist you in your efforts to return your abducted child to his or her country of habitual residence.
    - http://www.fbi.gov/scams-safety/fraud/internet_fraud
    a. **How to file a complaint** - The IC3 accepts online Internet crime complaints from either the actual victim or from a third party to the complainant. We can best process your complaint if we receive accurate and complete information from you.
    - http://www.ic3.gov/default.aspx

VI. **U.S Embassy**

  A. **List of U.S. Embassies Around the World** – Directory of US Embassies and consulates around the globe.
  - http://www.usembassy.gov/

Philippines

I. **Philippine Embassies**

    A. **Embassies and Consulates** – List of Philippine Embassies and Consulates around the world.
        - http://www.cfo.gov.ph/index.php?option=com_we blinks&view=category&id=152&Itemid=849

    B. **Consular Services** - Passport Information, Authentication Information and Visa Information
        - https://www.dfa.gov.ph/index.php/site-administrator

II. **US Embassy**

    A. **Official Website** - http://manila.usembassy.gov/

    B. **Visas** - http://manila.usembassy.gov/visas.html

    C. **US Citizens Services** - http://manila.usembassy.gov/service.html

III. **Bureau of Immigration**

The Bureau administers and enforces the immigration, citizenship and alien registration laws of the Philippines.

    A. **Contact Information**
        - http://immigration.gov.ph/index.php?option=com_c ontent&task=view&id=129&Itemid=73

    B. **Satellite Office Locations** – List of Bureau of Immigrations Local Offices
        - http://www.livingincebuforums.com/ipb/topic/ 13659-philippines-bureau-of-immigration-satellite-office-locations/

    C. **Visa Services – Head Office**
        1. **Immigrant Visa**
            - http://immigration.gov.ph/index.php?option=com_ content&task=view&id=26&Itemid=35
        2. **Non-Immigrant Visa**

      - http://immigration.gov.ph/index.php?option=com_
      content&task=view&id=25&Itemid=36

3. **Dual Citizenship**
      -http://immigration.gov.ph/index.php?option=com_
      content&task=view&id=163&Itemid=83

4. **Student Desk**
      - http://immigration.gov.ph/index.php?option=com_
      content&task=view&id=1743&Itemid=146

IV. **Department of Tourism**

The primary Philippine government agency charged with the responsibility to encourage, promote and develop tourism as a major socio-economic activity to generate foreign currency and employment and to spread the benefits of tourism to both the private and public sector.

A. **Contact Information -**
http://www.tourism.gov.ph/SitePages/contactus.aspx

B. **Philippine Tourism** – Department of Tourism official website
- http://www.tourism.gov.ph/Pages/default.aspx

1. **List of overseas offices -**
http://www.tourism.gov.ph/SitePages/overseasoffic es.aspx

2. **List of regional offices -**
http://www.tourism.gov.ph/SitePages/regoffices.as px

C. **Doing Business in the Philippines** - Anyone, regardless of nationality, is welcome to invest in the Philippines. With the liberalization of the foreign investment law, 100% foreign equity may be allowed in all areas of investment except those reserved for Filipinos by mandate of the Philippine Constitution and existing laws.
- http://www.tourism.gov.ph/SitePages/doingbusiness.a spx

V. **Department of Trade**

   A. **Regional Offices** – List of Regional Offices across the Philippines.
     - http://www.dti.gov.ph/dti/index.php?p=140

   B. **Consumer Welfare** – Know the exact agency to contact according to your concern as a consumer.
     - http://www.dti.gov.ph/dti/index.php?p=68

   C. **E-Mail Scam** – How to avoid being scammed and where to report a scam incident.
     - http://www.dti.gov.ph/dti/index.php?p=645

VI. **Department of Interior & Local Government**

The Department of Interior & Local Government (DILG) assists the office of the president in the exercise of general supervision over local government (LGUs).

   A. **Contact Information -**
     http://www.dilg.gov.ph/keyofficials.php

   B. **Local Government Units** – Roster of Local Government Units and their respective leaders.
     - http://www.dilg.gov.ph/lgu.php

   C. **DILG Regional Offices** – List of the department's regional offices
     - http://www.dilg.gov.ph/keyofficials.php

VII. **National Bureau of Investigation**

The National Bureau of Investigation (NBI) under the Department of Justice is the chief investigating arm of the government patterned after the Federal Bureau of Investigation (FBI)

   A. **Contact Information -**
     http://www.nbi.gov.ph/contact_us.html

   B. **Divisions** – The Bureau's list of divisions and directorates.

- http://www.nbi.gov.ph/divisions.html
C. **Regional & Field Offices** – List of Regional & Field offices across the Philippines
- http://www.nbi.gov.ph/field_offices.html

VIII.   **Philippine National Police**

The Philippine National Police or the PNP is the lead law enforcement agency of the Philippines. Its main task is enforce the law, prevent and control crimes, maintain peace and order and ensure public safety and internal security with the active support of the community.
A. **Contact Information** - http://edesk.pnp.gov.ph/
B. **PNP Regional Offices** – PNP Regional office directory
-http://pnp.gov.ph/portal/contact-us/rceo-telephone-numbers/94-protelephone/
729-pnp-police-regional-office-6-telephone-directory

IX.   **Other Government Agencies**

A. **National Statistics Office** - The National Statistics Office (NSO) is the major statistical agency responsible in collecting, compiling, classifying, producing, publishing and disseminating general-purpose statistics as provided for in Commonwealth Act (CA) No. 591. NSO has also the responsibility of carrying out and administering the provisions of the Civil Registry Law as provided for in Act No. 3753 dated February 1931.
- http://www.census.gov.ph/
1.   **Civil Registration** - Civil registry documents that can be obtained from the National Statistics Office. These include birth certificate, marriage certificate, death certificate and Certificate of No Marriage (CENOMAR). This section further discusses in detail the requirements and procedures in securing copies of

these documents.   -
http://www.census.gov.ph/civilregistration
B. **Philippine Postal Office** – The premiere postal service company of the Philippines
    - http://www.phlpost.gov.ph/web/

United Kingdom

A. **UK Embassies** - http://uk.embassyhomepage.com/
B. **British Embassy - Philippines**
- https://www.gov.uk/government/world/organisations/british-embassy-manila
C. **UK Border Agency** - The Home Office leads on immigration and passports, drugs policy, crime policy and counter-terrorism and works to ensure visible, responsive and accountable policing in the UK.
    - http://www.ukba.homeoffice.gov.uk/
D. **Anti-Fraud Agencies**
    1. **National Fraud Authority** - The National Fraud Authority (NFA) works with wider government, law enforcement, industry and voluntary/charity sectors to coordinate the fight against fraud in the UK.
       - https://www.gov.uk/government/organisations/national-fraud-authority/about
    2. **Action Fraud** - Action Fraud is the UK's national fraud and internet crime reporting centre
       We provide a central point of contact for information about fraud and financially motivated internet crime. If you've been scammed, ripped off or conned, there is something you can do about it. Report fraud to us and receive a police crime reference number.
       - http://www.actionfraud.police.uk/
    3. **Serious Fraud Office** - The Serious Fraud Office is an independent government department,

operating under the superintendence of the Attorney General. Its purpose is to protect society by investigating and, if appropriate, prosecuting those who commit serious or complex fraud, bribery and corruption and pursuing them and others for the proceeds of their crime. It operates in line with its statutory purpose and policies.

- http://www.sfo.gov.uk/

E. **Other Government Agencies**

A. **Office of Fair Trading** -Enforces consumer protection law and competition law, reviews proposed mergers and conducts market studies. Decisions and press notices.

- http://www.oft.gov.uk/

B. **Her Majesty's Passport Office** - HM Passport Office is the sole issuer of UK passports and responsible for civil registration services through the General Register Office. HM Passport Office is an executive agency of the Home Office

- https://www.gov.uk/government/organisations/hm-passport-office

1. **General Register Office** - is part of Her Majesty's Passport Office and oversees civil registration in England and Wales. We maintain the national archive of all births, marriages and deaths dating back to 1837

- http://www.gro.gov.uk/gro/content/

Canada

A. **Canadian Embassies -**
http://ca.embassyinformation.com/
  a. **Embassies and Consulates -**
http://travel.gc.ca/assistance/embassies

B. **Canadian Embassy – Philippines**
-http://www.canadainternational.gc.ca/
philippines/index.aspx

C. **Citizenship & Immigration Canada** – Canadian
Immigration
- http://www.cic.gc.ca/english/information/offices/

D. **Anti-Fraud Agencies**
1. **Canadian Anti-Fraud Centre** - The Canadian
Anti-Fraud Centre (CAFC) is the central agency in
Canada that collects information and criminal
intelligence on mass marketing fraud
(telemarketing), advance fee fraud letters (e.g. West
African), internet fraud and I.D theft complaints.
-http://www.antifraudcentre-
centreantifraude.ca/english/home.html

E. **Other Government Agencies**
1. **Foreign Affairs, Trade and Development
Canada** - The mandate of Foreign Affairs, Trade
and Development Canada is to manage Canada's
diplomatic and consular relations, to encourage
the country's international trade and to lead
Canada's international development and
humanitarian assistance.
- http://www.international.gc.ca/international/index
.aspx?lang=eng

2. **Genealogy Services** - (Records, Archives & Civil
Registry) The Genealogy Services' policy and
strategic priorities have been established to
improve service to Canadians. This is in
accordance with specific initiatives of the federal

government, namely Improving Service to Canadians and the Canadian Culture Online strategy.
   - http://www.collectionscanada.gc.ca/genealogy/index-e.html
3. **Passport Canada** - On July 2, 2013, Canada's Passport Program became integrated into Citizenship and Immigration Canada. As mandated by the Canadian Passport Order, the Passport Program's responsibilities include issuing, refusing to issue, revoking, withholding, recovering and providing instructions on the use of Canadian passports.
   - http://www.ppt.gc.ca/index.aspx

Australia

A. **Australian Embassies -**
   http://www.embassy.gov.au/
B. **Australian Embassy - Philippines**
   - http://www.philippines.embassy.gov.au/mnla/home.html
C. **Department of Immigration & Citizenship –** Australian Immigration
   - http://www.immi.gov.au/
D. **Births, deaths and marriages registries** - In Australia civil registrations are carried out and held by individual states. Information recorded in records varies from state to state. Most states call the appropriate central registry for the state the Office of the Registrar General of Births, Deaths and Marriages. In South Australia it is the Principal Registrar of Births, Deaths and Marriages and in Victoria it is the Government Statist Registry of Births, Deaths and Marriages.

-http://australia.gov.au/topics/law-and-justice/births-deaths-and-marriages-registries

E. **Australian Passport Office** - Department of Foreign Affairs
-https://www.passports.gov.au/Web/Requirements/IdentityDocuments.aspx

F. **Anti-Fraud Agencies**

   1. **Australian Government Services Fraud Tip-off** -The Australian Government Services Fraud Tip-off Line provides people with a place to report suspected fraud against Medicare, Centrelink and Child Support programs.
     - http://www.humanservices.gov.au/customer/information/fraud-and-security

   2. **Australian Crime Commission** - The Australian Crime Commission (ACC) is established under the Australian Crime Commission Act 2002 as a statutory authority to combat serious and organised crime. We report directly to the Minister for Home Affairs and are part of the Attorney-General's portfolio.
     - http://www.crimecommission.gov.au/organised-crime/fraud-and-financial-crime

   3. **Australian Competition Consumer Commission** – Scam reports and complaints.
     -http://australia.gov.au/service/scams-reports-and-complaints

   4. **Australian Federal Police** –Internet Fraud and Scams
     - http://www.afp.gov.au/policing/cybercrime/internet-fraud-and-scams.aspx

New Zealand

A. **New Zealand Embassies -**
    http://www.nzembassy.com/
B. **New Zealand Embassy - Philippines**
    - http://www.nzembassy.com/philippines
C. **Immigration New Zealand -** Immigration New Zealand is responsible for bringing the best people to New Zealand to enhance New Zealand's social and economic outcomes. We directly support labour market growth by attracting the best people to New Zealand and supporting them into the workforce so they become long-term contributors. We also contribute to key export industries like tourism and education.
    - http://www.immigration.govt.nz/
D. **Department of Internal Affairs -** New Zealand Government historical records for births, deaths and marriages are available to search online.
    -http://www.dia.govt.nz/Births-deaths-and-marriages
E. **New Zealand Passports** – Application and renewal of passport under the Department of Internal Affairs.
    - http://www.passports.govt.nz/
F. **Anti-Fraud Agencies**
    1. **Department of Internal Affairs: Anti-Scam** –Anti-Scam & Anti-Spam as reported to the Department's Electronic Messaging Compliance Team.
        - http://www.dia.govt.nz/Services-Anti-Spam-Reported-Scams
    2. **New Zealand Police: Anti-Spam Unit** – Handles Internet Scams and Fraud
        - http://www.police.govt.nz/safety/internet.scams.html

European Union

A. **List of diplomatic missions of the European Union**
   - http://en.wikipedia.org/wiki/List_of_diplomatic_m issions_of_the_European_Union
B. **EU embassies – Philippines**
   1. **Home Page & Contact Information**
      - http://eeas.europa.eu/delegations/philippines/ind ex_en.htm
   2. **List of EU embassies in the Philippines**
      - http://eeas.europa.eu/delegations/philippines/eu _travel/embassies/index_en.htm
C. **EU Immigration**
   1. **European Commission - EU Immigration Portal** - If you are a citizen of a country outside the European Union wishing to migrate to a country inside the European Union, then this site has useful information for you.
      - http://ec.europa.eu/immigration/
D. **European Civil Registry Network (ECRN)** - The ECRN project deals with the establishment of a pilot among the Civil Acts Registry of National Administrations to allow safe transmission and certain identification of the Civil Acts exchanged among European administrations.
   - http://www.ecrn.eu/BBB/index.php?lang=en
E. **Anti-Fraud Agencies**
   1. **European Anti-Fraud Office** –EU fraud investigative body.
      -http://ec.europa.eu/anti_fraud/about-us/mission/index_en.htm
   2. **Europol – EC3 -** Following a feasibility study conducted by Rand Corporation Europe, the European Commission decided to establish a European Cybercrime Centre (EC3) at Europol.

> The Centre will be the focal point in the EU's fight against cybercrime, contributing to faster reactions in the event of online crimes. It will support Member States and the European Union's institutions in building operational and analytical capacity for investigations and cooperation with international partners.
> - https://www.europol.europa.eu/ec3

Japan

A. **Japanese Embassies -**
   http://www.mofa.go.jp/about/emb_cons/mofaserv.html

B. **Japanese Embassy - Philippines**
   - http://www.ph.emb-japan.go.jp/

C. **Japanese Immigration Bureau** – Japanese immigration services
   - http://www.immi-moj.go.jp/english/

D. **Anti-Fraud Agencies**
   1. **Japan Company Trust Organization** – Anti-fraud Organization in Japan
      - http://www.japancompanytrust.org/complaints/
   2. **National Police Agency** – Japan's national police handles all internet related crimes or cybercrime.
      - http://www.npa.go.jp/english/index.htm

E. Non-Government Organization
   1. **Association of Foreign Wives of Japanese (AFWJ)** – Support Group. Processing of passport and civil registry documents.
      - http://www.afwj.org/resources.html

FOR MORE INFORMATION, PLEASE VISIT WWW.GLOBALFIANCE.COM TODAY!